EMBRACING THE DAWN

*Journey of Healing
Through the Darkness*

Fe Anam Avis

soul shop

Embracing The Dawn

Journey of Healing Through the Darkness

(previously published as Dawnings: Daily Scripture for those on the Path of Healing from Suicidal Thinking)

Published by True Potential

ISBN (print): 9781960024428

ISBN (ebook): 9781960024435

LCCN: 2024942431

True Potential

REACH THE WORLD

True Potential, Inc.

PO Box 904, Travelers Rest, SC 29690

www.truepotentialmedia.com

Produced and Printed in the United States of America.

Dedicated to:
Michelle Snyder
and
Christopher Epperson

CONTENTS

PREFACE

I have written this book out of my direct, personal experience with suicidal thinking.

Though I had served as a pastor for several years and conducted services for persons who had died by suicide, I had never reflected on the nature of suicidal thinking. I suppose I had a vague sense that some kind of mysterious chemical, neurological, or spiritual malady overtook an otherwise normal person and made them want to die.

Then, during an extremely stressful transition in my life in August 1984, I began to consider suicide myself for the first time. I lived with that possibility for about two months, long enough for it to establish a root in my psyche. It gradually began to fade as the pain and isolation of my situation began to ease. I now realize it simply went dormant.

It reemerged about a decade later as new problems presented themselves that seemed both unsolvable and inescapable. However, instead of manifesting itself as a mental intention and plan to kill myself, I began to have distressing mental images that were unbidden and unstoppable.

A major shift took place during a two-year divorce process. Now, I was actively considering ways to kill myself. In reflection, the reasons why seemed obvious. My life was falling apart. I was 51 years old and broke. All my earthly possessions were loaded into my car. I was essentially homeless, and would have been living in a shelter were it not for the kindness of an older couple who took me in and allowed me to live in their basement. Contempt of court charges had been filed against me with the expressed hope that I would be sent to jail. None of my four children would speak to me. My mother had cut off all communication with me as well. People I had known well would silently pass me on the street, pretending not to see me.

In November 2003, I found myself at a gun counter to purchase the weapon I would use to kill myself. At the last moment, I decided instead to check myself into the emergency department at The Ohio State University Hospital. I walked up to the person at the intake desk and simply said, "I need help. I'm planning to kill myself."

Things happened quickly. They removed anything from my clothing that I might use to harm myself, belt, shoe strings, ink pens, etc., and placed me in a room with soft walls. They screened me for symptomology with a series of questions. They did not seem very interested in what was actually happening in my life.

A pair of them diagnosed me as suffering from a major depressive disorder, prescribed medication, developed a safety plan, and set up an appointment with a psychiatrist. They called one of my friends to meet with the three of us. Then, they discharged me.

The profound crises in my life, the multiple losses, the isolation by friends and loved ones, the legal threats, and the financial destitution all had been reduced to a mental illness with a pharmacological fix.

Over the decades since, I have discovered that this is the perspective of many in the helping professions regarding suicidal thinking. In this view, suicidal thinking is evidence of an underlying, untreated brain disorder that is primary. It then follows that if we simply treat the disorder, the suicidal impulse will diminish or disappear. In some cases, this works.

The advantages to an approach that assumes a problem located entirely in the mind or even the brain of the individual are obvious. It does not require an investment in knowing the person and the unbearable pain they are carrying, the reasons they feel trapped, and the ways they have become isolated. It does not require institutions, communities, and families to explore the ways they are contributing to the desperation, unintentionally in some cases but deliberately punitive in others. Putting a person on medication is so much easier than asking an entire community to change the way we deal with one another, whether we are talking about bullying in grade school or shunning in small towns.

Faith communities have responded in a variety of ways, but there are two major streams of thought. The more progressive ones have tended to acquiesce to the illness model, which compartmentalizes suicidal thinking, relegates it to the realm of the professional, and retreats from any significant role in facilitating a suicidal person's recovery. More conservative faith communities tend to view suicide through the lens of sin, repentance, and forgiveness. Whether intended or not, the shame of this approach often contributes to the stigma that drives the conversation underground without addressing the suicidal desperation at its root.

Suicidal thinking is the result of multiple factors. One of those factors is the experience of unbearable, inescapable, and isolating pain. This devotional assumes that suicide is a means of coping with that pain. Suicidal thinking is an honest, respectable attempt of an individual to solve a problem or to at least live with an unsolvable problem in the comfort that there is a way out if they need it. In this sense, it is similar to other coping mechanisms, alcohol, over- or under-eating, over-shopping, etc.

Carl Jung said the craving for alcohol was "the equivalent of the spiritual thirst for wholeness." I have come to believe that suicidal thinking is the equivalent of a spiritual thirst for peace, clarity, and love. Like alcoholism, recovery from suicidism[1] requires the slow, steady healing and rebuilding of the inner life. Medications may be an element of that process. But the daily spiritual drip of love, challenge, and hope is essential to a positive outcome.

This is precisely the purpose of this book.

---

1   The quality or state of being suicidal.

INTRODUCTION

"Why is light given to the miserable, and life to the bitter of soul, who long for death that does not come, and search for it like hidden treasure, who rejoice and greatly exult when they can find the grave?" -- Job 3:20-22

The story of Job provides the quintessential Old Testament description of suicidal thinking. For those of us who wrestle with thoughts of suicide, its forty-two chapters resonate with nearly every element of our experience: the multiple unbearable losses, the well-intentioned but unhelpful friends, the impatience of spouses and partners, the questions about why God is allowing this to happen, the inability to find relief in either waking or sleeping.

The one difference is that Job is able to be more honest than most of us feel we can be. He is straightforward about his thoughts of suicide: "I would rather be strangled—rather die [hang myself] than suffer like this." (Job 7:15, NLT) The honesty of his mortal struggle does not diminish the power of his witness. In fact, it makes his eventual recovery even more credible.

In the end, Job does not kill himself. He not only survives his ordeal; he emerges into a life that is significantly reinvented. Like any reinvented person, he must learn to live with many irretrievable losses of the past without allowing those losses to poison the beauty of each new day.

We live in a society that resists an honest conversation about the suicidal experience and the hopeful process of recovering from that darkest of nights. Gratefully, the Bible hides neither the pain nor the promise of that journey. Suicide, suicidal thinking, and the healing power of God's love are brought into plain view in many of the Bible's pages. In the honest descriptions of that pain, we find assurance that we are not alone. In the deliverance of persons from their agonized thinking, we find hope that we, also, can indeed recover to find lives worth living.

The unbearable circumstances of life can reduce even the strongest and most accomplished to a point where they are unable to claim their own dignity as human beings. Their emotional, spiritual, and physical reserves are significantly depleted. They are weakened by the inner abscesses of confusion, shame, guilt, and self-doubt.

When all was going well, Job appeared to be faultless. However, under the stress of his multiple losses, Job was revealed to be no invincible saint. None of us is. Today, persons with suicidal thoughts are characterized in a variety of ways, some of which are true, some half-true, but many outright falsehoods. Like the rest of society, we are simply imperfect human beings and imperfect in similar ways.

Nonetheless, in many faith communities we have been silenced by shame to the point of invisibility, a kind of emotional exile. We will meet other exiled souls, a thousand years after Job, in the ministry of Jesus. Oddly enough, it is these stigmatized persons who are the very ones that Jesus befriended, forgave, and healed, a veritable VIP list of the New Testament.

This book of daily scriptures is focused on that healing process. It is not designed to be a replacement for the services of mental health professionals when those are needed. It is my experience that recovering from suicidal thinking requires an array of resources customized to the individual. This book is only one element of a larger recovery plan that might include family, friends, physicians, mental health professionals, mentors, and, in some cases, medication.

However, recovering from suicidal thinking requires more than a pill and a pat on the back, as important as these can be. It requires a change in thinking, what the Bible calls "metanoia." This simply cannot be accomplished short of a regular "updating" of our mental and spiritual processes, daily, if possible. God brings us out of the dark shadows of suicide one step at a time.

My experience of suicidal thinking is similar to that of living through a very dark night, what John of the Cross referred to as the dark night of the soul. With the right help, a new day begins to gradually dawn. Like all sunrises, the day breaks slowly at first, almost imperceptively. One cannot be certain if that faint glow in the east is real or a desperately wished-for improvement. With time, it becomes certain that things are improving, and life may be worth living after all.

The process isn't always a straight line. We may be plunged into the darkness multiple times, but each time, we become more confident that a new day will eventually dawn. The title of this book, *Embracing The Dawn,* reflects the multiple nights and day breaks that are part of a typical recovery process.

The title is also intended to reflect the importance of spiritual insight for our recovery process. "And then it dawned on me" is a phrase we use to describe an important thought or idea that breaks through into our consciousness. Even though it may be something we have read or heard from someone else, it feels like it comes from beyond them. Much as the sun illumines the earth from millions of miles away, when something "dawns on us," it feels like a message that has come to us from out of this world, from God.

Suicidal thinking is not the end of Job's story, nor need it be ours. At the close of the last chapter, we are told that "All his brothers and sisters and everyone who had known him before came and ate with him in his house. They comforted and consoled him over all the trouble the Lord had brought on him, and each one gave him a piece of silver and a gold ring. The Lord blessed the latter part of Job's life more than the former part."

If we can allow ourselves to move past the culturally conditioned imagery of these verses into what they symbolize, the message is clear. The goal of our recovery process goes far beyond mere survival. The goal is nothing less than abundant living. At the beginning of our recovery, this is unfathomable. However, I can now bear witness to scores of people who have walked this road out of the darkest of nights, and they would repeat these simple words of hope: "I'm so grateful I stayed alive to see these days. I wouldn't have missed them for the world."

Using this Book

I created this book for those who find insight, inspiration, and strength in what Christians refer to as the Old and New Testaments. It is not required that a person be a member of a particular faith tradition or faith community to benefit from these daily readings.

It will be helpful to use this book as a daily spiritual practice. However, don't let perfectionism sabotage your recovery. If you miss a day or two, simply begin again where you left off. Always, we begin again.

These readings are ordered with the goal of recovery in mind. They follow a sequence that is intentional. You will likely find it more helpful to follow them in order than to jump into them at random.

People experience suicidal thinking in a variety of ways, and the recovery process will be different for each person. Some readings will relate to you more than others. Don't let that stop you. Remember that while it may not relate to you, it relates to others like you. In those cases, take a moment to pray for them or to hold them in your heart with loving intention.

As you engage these readings, it is important to exercise faith in your own healing process. That involves a degree of patient realism. Suicidal thinking doesn't usually develop overnight, and it doesn't retreat quickly. We must keep doing our daily readings and give the Spirit time.

As I mentioned earlier in the introduction, this book is not intended to serve as your sole recovery resource. As you engage in the daily readings, it may be helpful for you to have one or two persons you trust with whom you can share your reactions. Speaking your thoughts out loud to someone who is really listening almost always clarifies your thinking.

Sadly, some people have had such traumatic experiences in faith communities of the past that a book such as this unintentionally triggers painful memories. What God intends to be healing is twisted into something harmful. If you find that happening, put the book aside and find other resources to help you.

A final, necessary word about safety. Should you find at any point that you are on the verge of harming yourself or another, put this book down and get help immediately. Call the suicide hotline. **That number is 988.**

THE RECOVERY PRAYER

Healer of my Soul,

I surrender to your greater purposes in my life, to what I must lose for what I might gain, that in your Divine hands, the weight of this unbearable burden might become a liberating force, breaking the bonds of hopelessness and unleashing my Soul to the work of creating a life truly worth living.

Amen.

DAY ONE

As he passed by, he saw a man blind from birth. And his disciples asked him, "Rabbi, who sinned, this man or his parents, that he was born blind?" Jesus answered, "It was not that this man sinned, or his parents, but that the works of God might be displayed in him. We must work the works of him who sent me while it is day; night is coming, when no one can work. As long as I am in the world, I am the light of the world." Having said these things, he spit on the ground and made mud with the saliva. Then he anointed the man's eyes with the mud and said to him, "Go, wash in the pool of Siloam" (which means Sent). So, he went and washed and came back seeing.
-- John 9:1-7

Today, we begin a healing journey. The fact that you have picked up this book and started reading is a step of courage. Even if you read no further than this sentence and put the book down to be picked up later, you have taken a step toward recovery.

Our inspiration to begin is found in a man who was born blind over two thousand years ago. He will eventually receive his sight, but not immediately. It is reasonable to assume that Jesus could have healed him instantly as he had healed others, but he does not. Instead, Jesus asks him to begin his healing journey by walking blind, the same way he had walked the many years of his life.

For those of us who are struggling with thoughts of suicide, our healing journey often begins in just this way. We must take the first steps toward healing even while we are plagued with thoughts about taking our own lives. As the man in today's passage had to take his first step toward healing while still blind, we must take our first step toward healing while we are still struggling with inner pain and uncertainty.

That first step is the simple acknowledgment that life has become unlivable. Life, as we are living it, is killing us. Something must change. When your life is on the line, everything must go onto the table. You are worth that much.

The world is asking you to please stop thinking about suicide. But your soul, that deepest, most sacred part, is asking you to please admit that your life is unlivable and begin to create one that is. This will involve change.

But change how?

There are scores of voices trying to get your ear and dozens of hands tugging at your sleeve, pulling you this way and that, crying out, "Please, please, don't disappoint us, don't change your life too much, don't rock our boat." But when your life is on the line, only one voice matters: the voice of the God who created you and loves you unconditionally.

The disciples were tempted to engage in a debate about who to blame for the man's suffering. You may hear similar fault-finding conversations about your suffering. Jesus quickly turned these aside as irrelevant.

There were persons in the crowd with their own agendas who would have preferred that the man in our reading follow the religious conventions of his day, even if it meant remaining blind. He could not allow those voices to dissuade him from taking that step. Were he to fall to the temptation of craving their approval, he would have died blind just as he had been born blind.

No. He had to rise to his feet and start walking blind, mud dripping down his face, and heading for a promised healing at a destination he could not yet see. It was God's job to heal him. It was his job to start walking.

Today, we are invited to take that step. We may not be able to see the destination, but one thing is crystal clear: life has become unlivable. Only God can be trusted to guide us in creating a life worth living. We are worth that much.

It is God's job to heal us. It is our job to start walking. By reading this devotional and praying the following prayer, you have already started.

Welcome to our community.

Something to think about:

What do you think are your first steps in this journey, and Why? Is there someone who would be a good partner in this journey, and why?

Prayer

Jesus, I admit that my life has become unlivable, and I am tempted to believe that my unlivable life means that I should no longer live. Like a blind person, I have failed to see another possibility, that something in my life must die, *but not me.* I now put everything on the table for you to take up or set aside. I take the first step with you in this journey of healing. Amen.

"Every new beginning begins with some other beginning's end." – *Seneca*

DAY TWO

"When the disciples heard this, they were greatly surprised and asked, 'How can anyone ever be saved?' Jesus looked straight at them and said, 'There are some things people cannot do, but God can do anything.'" -- Matt. 19:25-26 (CEV)

Today's verses follow a statement by Jesus that it is very difficult for a rich person to enter a heaven-touched life (literally "the kingdom of heaven"). Notice that the problem is not with the door; God does not lock people out. The problem is with the *entering*. Some people simply cannot bring themselves to walk through the door into a better life. In fact, Jesus says it is virtually impossible for many people to succeed.

For those on the road to recovery from an unlivable-life to a life-worth-living, it is important for us to understand the impact of what Jesus is saying: you will likely not be able to do this on your own. In the words of the television stunt man disclaimer, "don't try this at home."

The disciples were astonished to hear this; the Greek word "astonished" literally means to go into shock or panic. We may have a similar reaction. Is this an exaggeration? Is it really the case that it is almost impossible to recover from suicidal thinking and enter a heaven-touched life without Divine help?

No, it is not an exaggeration. Yes, it is virtually impossible to recover from suicidal thinking without Divine help and the many different forms that Divine help will take as it is sent our way. It may be possible to simply keep oneself alive for decades through force of will or cling to mere survival by one's fingernails. However, this is a poor substitute for the abundant life that Jesus promised or the love, joy, and peace that the Apostle Paul identifies as the qualities of a life in Christ.

At the beginning of their recovery process, it is very difficult for people to hear talk about the joys of a life worth living. They are in too much pain. I have had numerous people tell me that they stopped reading my book, *A Second Day,* at the halfway point because it began to be hopeful...and they couldn't handle hope. They just could not enter a heaven-touched, life-worth-living, what Jesus calls the kingdom of heaven.

"God can do anything," Jesus promises. God can give us hope. God can guide us. God can heal us. God can straighten out our confused thinking. God can give us peace. God can reveal solutions to problems we cannot solve on our own. God can give us courage. However, we must not try to do heaven's work by human might. This will simply boomerang us back to another version of an un-livable life.

It is impossible to anticipate exactly how God is going to show up in our lives; that is personalized for each individual. We will discover God's unique way of working in our particular situation only by committing ourselves to God's purposes and then staying alert to the ways we are being aided.

There are some things people can't do, but God can do anything. The door to a heaven-touched, life-worth-living stands open. A warm welcome awaits you. Make the commitment. Enter.

Something to think about:

What are some ways you are open to God's divine help? What are some ways we can look at this door and our openness to enter?

Prayer:

Jesus, my life has become unlivable, and it is be-yond my power to make it a life worth living. But you can do anything. At this moment, without terms or conditions, I commit my life into your hands. By your grace, let a new day dawn. Open my eyes to recognize your work in the days ahead. I say again: you can do anything. Amen.

Until one is committed, there is hesitancy, the chance to draw back, and always ineffectiveness. Concerning all acts of initiative and creation, there is one elementary truth the ignorance of which kills countless ideas and splendid plans: that the moment one definitely commits oneself, then providence moves too.

All sorts of things occur to help one that would never otherwise have occurred. A whole stream of events issues from the decision, raising in one's favor all manner of unforeseen incidents, meetings, and material assistance which no one could have dreamed would have come his way. Begin it now. – *Goethe*

DAY THREE

"But when Ahijah heard the sound of her feet, as she came in at the door, he said, 'Come in, wife of Jeroboam. Why do you pretend to be another? For I am charged with unbearable news for you.'" -- 1 Kgs. 14:6

In today's reading, a mother whose son is ill comes to Ahijah, the prophet, to learn her son's fate. He delivers the news that every mother dreads: her child will not survive. The emotional impact of this news is unmistakable. The word used in the reading is "unbearable."

The widespread misconception regarding those of us who are contemplating suicide is that we are simply mentally ill and only need to be medicated or even institutionalized. This is a gross misrepresentation. Research reveals that the vast majority of us who are struggling with suicidal thinking are dealing with something *unbearable*, often a circumstance that has overwhelmed us.

That unbearable circumstance may be a collection of many things that have accumulated over months or years, but, like this mother in today's reading, it is often one or two unbearable things on which we are focused:

☐ The death of someone dear to us.

☐ A painful divorce or other relationship loss.

☐ The loss of a job or a financial crisis.

☐ An arrest or other legal issue.

☐ A damaged reputation.

☐ Being bullied or harassed.

☐ Being estranged from one's friends and family.

☐ The diagnosis of a debilitating disease or a series of diagnoses.

The Bible is straightforward on this point. Its pages are filled with accounts of many who face unbearable circumstances, a number of whom consider, attempt, or die by suicide. These are not defective, sick persons, nor are they isolated cases. They are not difficult to understand. In virtually every case, we can list the unbearable circumstances that brought them to this point.

Naming the unbearable in our lives is an essential part of our recovery process. We can begin by naming those unbearable circumstances to ourselves, perhaps even writing them down. The next step in the healing process would be to speak those things to another person whom we trust will not judge us or try to minimize our pain.

Finally, and perhaps most importantly, we can turn to the God who will never leave us hopeless and forsaken. The New Testament word "gospel" literally means "good news." That good news, given such rich expression in the life and ministry of Jesus, is that God's ultimate purposes for us are healing and wholeness. Like the mother in today's reading, we will all face unbearable news, some so devastating we may begin to despair about life itself.

This does not make us weak or pitiable. It *does* number us with the millions of others who have found themselves in daily need of the good news of God's healing love. There is no unbearable news that the world can give us that can outmatch the good news of God's healing power. We must summon as much faith as we can muster in response. That is always enough in the kingdom of heaven.

Something to think about:

When thinking about having a conversation with someone or "speaking in the direction" of someone I trust, what are those things that you find unbearable? Why? Can God be included in this conversation?

Prayer

God, I have found myself crushed by one or several unbearable burdens in my life. Like the mother in the Bible, I can still remember the moment I received that unbearable news. Yet, you have not left me hopeless, for the good news of your love is that Jesus has come to bring healing to the brokenhearted. I do not yet know how I will be healed, but I open my heart and mind, my body and soul to that good news, trusting that I will be made whole in your time. Amen.

DAY FOUR

Now in those days the counsel that Ahithophel gave was as if one consulted the word of God; so was all the counsel of Ahithophel esteemed...-- 2 Sam. 16:23

When Ahithophel saw that his counsel was not followed, he saddled his donkey and went off home to his own city. He set his house in order and hanged himself, and he died and was buried in the tomb of his father.-- 2 Sam. 17:23

An anonymous author wrote that if you can't be a good example, you'll just have to be a horrible warning. The life of Ahithophel is a cautionary tale. He is in the Bible to teach us what not to do and how not to be.

We know little about Ahithophel. Did he have a wife or children, like King David did? We don't know. Did he love music like King Saul? No idea. Did he have friends? The Bible doesn't say. Did he believe in God? Nothing there either.

Actually, we know only one thing about Ahithophel. We know that he was an advisor to King David. And, apparently, he was extremely good at his job -- "so was all the counsel of Ahithophel esteemed." Ahithophel found great purpose in his work. One of the things we know about suicide is that having a meaningful purpose, such as work, is protective against suicide. It provides a reason for living, keeps us connected to others, and is a source of self-esteem.

However, when all we have is a single protective factor, we are vulnerable to its loss. Master suicide intervention trainer, Melissa Witmeier, points out how quickly a single protective factor can become a risk factor.

"Animals can be an important source of mental health," Witmeier teaches, "and a beloved pet can be protective against suicide. However, the death of that pet can suddenly put the pet's owner at risk. They can begin thinking of suicide."

How often have I seen it happen that a single, positive focus in a person's life leaves them vulnerable upon its loss. A man finds his entire life's purpose in his work, excels, and earns the respect of friends and colleagues. But retirement is a blow that is difficult to navigate. A woman makes a similar singular investment in raising children. But when they leave home, or worse, estrange her, she feels she has lost all reason to live.

Notice that it is something positive and worthwhile that becomes the occasion for our suicidal thinking upon its loss. We are told that "the counsel Ahithophel gave was as if one consulted the word of God." But when a bad decision on his part brought his work to an end, he had nothing left except suicide.

Some of us who are recovering from suicidal thinking find ourselves in a similar place. There were some things we were very good at: work, parenting, sports, and art. Or a relationship that was extremely important to us. Through that aspect of our lives, we made a positive contribution, expanded our character, and changed lives for the better.

Then it was gone. We feel devastated as a result. Like Ahithophel, we may see no reason for living, and we may find it hard to imagine that can ever change.

But it can. Millions of us have gone through this dark night of the soul. We lingered on the edge of suicide or may even have harmed ourselves in some way. We are here to bear witness to the fact that the darkness can lift and light can return to your life.

As we will see in the readings ahead, we do not need to take the Ahithophel's fork in the road. We are larger than any job, and we are more than any single relationship. We are children of God. With God's help, we can "walk through the valley of the shadow of death," not fall into it.

You are a box of crayons. Give God time to bring all the other colors to your life. Give God time.

Something to think about:

What are some protective factors in your life? What are those concrete examples?

PrayerGod of Hope, you see my life through the prism of possibilities while I am experiencing life through the lens of loss. Give me strength as I walk through this season of pain, but also give me hope that daylight will eventually break through this dark night. I choose to give you time to work your healing in my life, one day at a time. In the meantime, I will keep reaching out to the help that I need, the people, the professionals, and the positive messages of rebirth and renewal. Amen.

DAY FIVE

And the LORD God formed man of the dust of the ground, and breathed into his nostrils the breath of life; and man became a living soul.-- Gen. 2:7 (KJV)

Why are you cast down, O my soul, and why are you in turmoil within me? Hope in God; for I shall again praise him, my salvation and my God.-- Ps. 43:5

The earliest creation story is not found in our book of Genesis but in the writings of an ancient people called the Sumerians, dating back to the third millennium BC. According to the Sumerians, human beings were only created to serve as a labor force. All that mattered was their physical ability to do work so that the Sumerian gods could be freed from their toil. What humans thought, felt, or chose was superfluous.

In contrast, the book of Genesis depicts God creating us as *living souls*. These souls are given life when the breath of God enters a human body. God and humans share the same inner breath. It is this shared inner breath that makes us human, makes us living souls.

A remarkable aspect of the God revealed in the Bible is that God cares for our souls, that inner quality of life that energizes our thoughts, feelings, and will. Verses like today's reading, "Why are you cast down, O my soul," make it into the Bible because that inner state of how we think and feel matters.

This means that when it comes to the topic of suicide, God cares about more than our outer actions. When someone says, "Yes, I think about killing myself, but I would never do it," that is simply not good enough for God. The fact that someone is living in such a state of inner despair matters, even if we never become a statistic by self-injuring or taking our own life.

If the number of suicides and suicide attempts were reduced to zero, that would fulfill the missions of most suicide prevention organizations in the United States. But God cares about the Soul. Leaving people to an inner conversation where they are saying to themselves, "I loathe my life;" (Job 10:1) is simply not good enough.

We are a community of people who are recovering from suicidal thinking. Of course, we want to prevent actions that would lead to death or injury, but we want to do more than that. We want to care for our souls. This is the birthright of every church or spiritual community. The mission of social agencies may end when the body is safely sheltered, clothed, and fed. The purpose of the church goes to the heart of our inner life.

Among other things, this means that we do not use sharp distinctions between feeling, thinking, and acting as an excuse for neglecting that inner life. When someone says, "I don't want to live anymore, but I would never take my life," they are still in need of recovery.

In fact, there is an inner state I would call "suicide by giving up." GUI, "give-up-it is," refers to a researched condition of those who develop extreme apathy, give up hope, relinquish the will to live, and die despite no obvious organic cause. God cares about those of us on the verge of suicide by giving up even if we have no plan or means to physically take our lives.

We hear these days about those who, for one reason or another, want to die, but not at their own hand. They set up a situation where someone else kills them. The most common example is called "suicide by cop." But we see forms of this in the Bible as well. Jonah enlists the sailors on his ship to toss him overboard, "suicide by sailor." King Saul tries to order his armor-bearer to kill him, "suicide by a subordinate."

Then there are those who so despair of life that they pray that God will take their lives. Instances of these are found in the Bible as well, a kind of "suicide by prayer." The stigma attached to suicide has contributed to an avoidance of such straightforward talk.

The point is simply this: God cares about our souls. When the inner springs of life have been so depleted that we would rather die than live, we need healing. Whether by our own hand, the hand of another, the hand of God, or simply the slow deterioration of the body from a heart that has lost its verve is a rather limp distinction.

For the Psalmist, living in a permanent cast-down, tumultuous inner state is not an option. "Hope in God; for I shall again praise him, my salvation and my God."

He sets his intention on recovery. Let us join him—together.

Something to think about:

Are there times you feel like giving up? What are some things that can help shift your focus and attention toward God as a living soul?

PrayerJesus, Lover of my Soul, I give thanks that I am more than a laborer in your eyes. You care for my Soul, my inner life, the one I often neglect, hide, or even fear. Whatever the path that has brought me to this point, I will not be satisfied to simply exist or to finish my years with gritted teeth and a forced "hello." I submit myself to you, who loves me, heals me, and who will once again restore me to the joy of living. Amen.

DAY SIX

Cast your burden on the LORD, and he will sustain you.-- Ps. 55:22

The promise of God found in today's reading is that God "will sustain you." A more complete translation might be: "God will continue feeding and nourishing your inner life without fail." Suicidal thinking strangles our inner life. It threatens to emotionally starve us by choking off our spiritual food supply of love and hope. We cannot live without love. We cannot survive without hope. The Psalmist invites us to be nourished by God.

This nourishment is without price, but it does require something of us. We must cast our burden on the Lord. The language is clear and concrete. The burden is the crushing weight of that unbearable circumstance that we carry, not only in our minds but also in our bodies.

Simply reading these words is not enough. We must take action. The verb "cast" is in the form of a strong command and visualizes forcefully throwing something to the ground. Physically enacting this verse by attaching our burden to an object and forcibly casting it away from us can be an embodied expression of faith. One way of doing this is by finding a hand-sized stone, writing "Unbearable" on it, and throwing it to the ground as hard as we can.

If we do not have access to such a stone or the physical health to throw it safely, write it on a piece of paper IN ALL CAPITAL LETTERS, and place it in an offering plate at a religious service.

In casting our burden on the Lord, we must set an intention not to continue carrying it as if God somehow needs our help. Solutions to problems can appear that we will never recognize if we don't let go. Joyce Meyer writes: "Turn your situation over to God. God can do more in a moment than you can do in a lifetime."

Apart from God, bearing the unbearable is unsustainable. It becomes more difficult to free ourselves from suicidal thinking when we are exhausted. We end up saying to ourselves, "I am too tired to go on." But when we cast our burden onto the Lord, as our day's reading promises, God will sustain us. We are freed to find strength in the truth of God, that we are profoundly and everlastingly loved.

Name what God is inviting you to cast onto God. Whether you write it on a stone or a piece of paper, only one thing is important. Give it up. Let it go. Throw it down.

Something to think about:

What is the list you would place on your stone or paper? What would it include?

Prayer

Loving God, I realize that the burden I bear has been multiplied by my insistence on carrying it alone. Whether by ignorance, by stubbornness, or by simple force of habit, I have allowed this crushing weight to fall totally on my shoulders. Today, I take the next step in my recovery process by forcefully casting this problem upon you that I have been able to neither solve nor bear. I now wait patiently for your sustaining love and guidance. Amen.

DAY SEVEN

About midnight Paul and Silas were pray-
ing and singing hymns to God, and the
prisoners were listening to them, and sud-
denly there was a great earthquake, so
that the foundations of the prison were
shaken. And immediately all the doors
were opened, and everyone's bonds were
unfastened. When the jailer woke and saw
that the prison doors were open, he drew
his sword and was about to kill himself,
supposing that the prisoners had escaped.
-- Acts 16:25-27

This account of the Philippian jailor's attempted
suicide follows a familiar pattern that is as old as
the Bible itself and as current as the daily news. A
person awakes in the morning to what they expect
will be a typical day. They go through all their normal routines. They get dressed, greet their loved
ones, eat their breakfast, and head out into their
day's activities.

Then, something unexpected happens that changes everything, something so devastating that they begin to consider taking an action that they may never have seriously contemplated before—killing themselves. Roughly 30% of those who die by suicide experienced a crisis in the previous two weeks.

For our jailor, it happened faster than that. Within a few minutes of this unexpected event, he has made a life-or-death decision. This also follows a pattern. Research has revealed that roughly a quarter of those who decide to make a serious suicide attempt think about it for less than five minutes before taking action.[2] Nearly half think about it for less than twenty minutes.

As persons recovering from suicidal thinking, we must respect the healing power of time. Otherwise, we risk making a tragic mistake based on inaccurate or incomplete information. The Philippian jailor is basing the decision to kill himself on his erroneous perception that his prisoners have escaped.

When we are dealing with the stress of unbearable circumstances, we are often not thinking clearly. Is it really true that no one cares about us? That the world would be better off without us? That we simply cannot find happiness after the loss of an important relationship? That there are no options to solve our problems other than suicide?

---

2   https://www.hsph.harvard.edu/means-matter/means-matter/duration/

Here is the truth. Twenty-four hours can totally change our answers to these questions. Or even a fraction of a second. Persons who have survived a suicide attempt after jumping off the Golden Gate Bridge often say that only a half-second after they jumped, midair, *they realized they had made a mistake.*

The Apostle Paul's intervention completely changed the jailor's answers, and in just a few seconds: "Do not harm yourself. We are all here." We never know when some version of "Paul" will walk into our lives. I have heard the stories of person after person who were convinced they had nothing to live for, but a phone call, a letter, an encounter with the natural world, a miraculous survival, or a Divine encounter significantly changed how they viewed themselves and their future.

Undoubtedly, there is someone reading this day's reflection who is in that two-week danger zone. Some crisis has just happened or is about to happen in the days ahead that is taking you to the brink. Or, you are standing in the very shoes of this jailor, sword drawn. Give God time to work. If you can't hold off the impulse to injure yourself, call the suicide hotline, 988, and talk with someone.

After making that call, stay with these daily readings for the next few weeks. You never know who might show up that will change how you think about everything.

Something to think about:

What are some ways we can give God time to work? What are things I do to hamper His work in me?

Prayer

God of my journey, I remember my Philippian jailor moment when the shadow of darkness fell across my Soul, threatening to extinguish all hope. Perhaps that moment was not so long ago, or perhaps it is a moment I dread in the days yet to come. With your help, I give you time to work your healing in my life, to clarify my thinking, to allow the intensity of panic or rage to cool, and to open possibilities that I cannot now imagine. Save me from a decision that I would regret were I alive just a few minutes more, and bring me into a future where I am grateful for days I easily might have missed. Work a miracle in my life. Amen

DAY EIGHT

And [Jesus] told this parable: "A man had a fig tree planted in his vineyard, and he came seeking fruit on it and found none. And he said to the vinedresser, 'Look, for three years now I have come seeking fruit on this fig tree, and I find none. Cut it down. Why should it use up the ground?' And he answered him, 'Sir, let it alone this year also, until I dig around it and put on manure. Then if it should bear fruit next year, well and good; but if not, you can cut it down.'" -- Luke 13:6-9

In this parable of Jesus, the landowner holds all the power over the tree growing on his property. With a word, he can have it destroyed. And he seems to have good reason to do so. The landowner calls his farmworker over. He is decisive:

"Cut it down."

God has entrusted incredible powers into the hands of human beings. Among those is the power of life and death. Any person can take their own life. We are the landowner. Our life is the tree. We hold the power to cut it down.

Like the landowner, we might be tempted to do so out of impatience. Such impatience would be understandable. Fig trees typically produce fruit twice a year, every year. The fig tree in question has failed to produce anything for three years, with six failures in total.

For most of us, three years is a long time to feel that our lives are absolutely fruitless. Someone has said that the meaning of a life worth living is work to do, someone to love, lessons to learn, experiences to share. Three years of nothing to do, no one to love, nothing to learn, and no experiences to share is a recipe for self-destruction. And yet, in their honest moments, there are millions of people today who would say just that.

That would be the tragic end of the tree were it not for one other character in our story: the farmworker. The farmworker goes to bat for the tree.

"There is nothing wrong with the tree," he argues. "It just needs to be properly cared for. Its roots need air, its sap needs to be sweetened, and its leaves need to be fed. Give me time. This tree is worth saving. You'll see."

And here is the surprise of the story. The lowly farmworker is God! We are the landowner, our life is the tree, and the farmworker fighting for our life is God. God is asking for time to nourish our life at its roots, to give it the air of regular spiritual practice, to nourish it with love, to find meaningful connections with others, and to grow in knowledge and compassion.

None of this can happen quickly. In contrast to the impulsiveness of the Philippian jailor, suicidal thinking can sometimes develop slowly. For many of us, often in spite of all appearances, our souls have been quietly falling into disrepair for years. In my case, I had been able to do the work of ministry, preaching, teaching, and publicly praying, but I had not been tending to my soul. Warning lights were flashing on the dashboard of my life, but I kept shutting off the alarms. Finally, I had to face the ultimate warning light as I stood at a counter to buy a gun to take my life.

We cannot reverse in an instant what neglect has caused over the years. We must give God time to work. The working of God is like the cultivation of seeds, Jesus said. Like this parable, his favorite images were taken from agriculture. We cannot rush our recovery process any more than we can rush the ripening of an apple. But before we can have ripe apples, we must make sure we do not cut down the apple tree.

It is here that the parable ends. We know what the farmworker God wants to do. We know the tree is worth saving; we know what it can do. The remaining question is this: "What does the landowner want to do?"

What will we do?

Something to think about:

If we are the experts in our own lives, how can the farmer help form our thoughts and decisions?

Prayer

God, Farmworker of my soul, I often feel that my life is fruitless and has been for a while. I keep hoping that the mere passage of time will make things better, but the years go by, and nothing changes. Help me love the tree of my life as much as you do. Whatever my responsibility for the neglect of the roots of my Soul, please forgive me. Guide me into fresh ways to nourish my life at its roots, even if those ways are unfamiliar and awkward. If you will give me patience, Lord, I will give you time. Deal.

DAY NINE

And they came to Jericho. And as he was leaving Jericho with his disciples and a great crowd, Bartimaeus, a blind beggar, the son of Timaeus, was sitting by the roadside. And when he heard that it was Jesus of Nazareth, he began to cry out and say, "Jesus, Son of David, have mercy on me!" And many rebuked him, telling him to be silent. But he cried out all the more, "Son of David, have mercy on me!" And Jesus stopped and said, "Call him." -- Mark 10:46-49

A number of years ago, I assisted a professor friend of mine in teaching an annual, graduate-level social work class focused on the international AIDS crisis. Most of my presentation was spent describing the work of founding a home for abandoned HIV-infected children in Honduras.

The conversation always energized the students. Eventually, the same question would surface.

"How do you go about starting such a project?"

I would always say, "You have to learn to ask for help. Do you know how to ask for help?"

Then, I would engage them in a simple exercise by asking them to take turns saying to the person next to them, "I need help. Would you please help me?"

There was always an awkward pause followed by puzzled facial expressions asking, "Are you serious?"

I was serious. They would eventually comply. Then, I would follow with this statement.

"You are in a profession where many people will be asking you for help. There is only one way you are going to be able to respond to them in an authentic, sustainable way: by knowing how to ask for help when *you* need it."

In today's reading, a blind man named Bartimaeus is asking Jesus for help. There is no way for him to do this delicately. Since he is blind, he can't easily make his way to Jesus and engage him in a discrete, face-to-face conversation. His only option is to call out from the roadside.

As the students in our class experienced, asking for help can feel uncomfortable. It even feels uncomfortable to observe someone else asking for help. Undoubtedly, this is why many rebuked Bartimaeus, telling him to be silent. The Greek tense of the verb "rebuke" suggests a continuing action. The crowd was repeatedly telling Bartimaeus to shut-up.

"Will you please shut up, Bartimaeus! Shut up!"

Bartimaeus knew how to ask for help. The crowd didn't. Bartimaeus experienced a healing. The crowd didn't.

If we are going to recover from suicidal thinking, we will need to learn to ask for help. That ask can take many forms, from friends, family members, faith community leaders, chaplains, therapists, medical professionals, or a suicide hotline (call 988). Most importantly, we must learn how to ask God for help.

Bartimaeus made himself visible. He was not ashamed of who he was. And neither must we be.

Something to think about:

What are practical ways you can ask for help? When do you find yourself needing this kind of help?

Prayer

Jesus, I thank you for heeding the voice of Bartimaeus as he called out for help, and the encouragement he offers all of us on this healing journey. By your grace, lift from me the additional burden of my pride, which only makes life more unbearable while depriving me of your healing power. I need help. Would you please help me? Thank you.

DAY TEN

And they called the blind man, saying to him, "Take heart. Get up; he is calling you." And throwing off his cloak, he sprang up and came to Jesus. And Jesus said to him, "What do you want me to do for you?" And the blind man said to him, "Rabbi, let me recover my sight." And Jesus said to him, "Go your way; your faith has made you well." And immediately he recovered his sight and followed him on the way. -- Mark 10:49-52

Today, we continue our reflection on the healing of blind Bartimaeus.

It doesn't require much of an imagination for us to envision the range of problems that blindness would bring into the life of a first-century Palestinian man. Vocationally, his daily job is begging. Economically, he is destitute. As we have seen, he is an embarrassment to his neighbors. Except for the briefest reference to his father, Timaeus, no family members are mentioned. His family and friends may have all fallen victim to compassion fatigue. We simply don't know.

When Jesus asks the wide-open question, "What do you want me to do for you," what might Bartimaeus ask for? Riches? Luxury? Mansions? Romance? Prestige? No, Bartimaeus asks to receive his sight, to be healed.

It is natural for us to want to be relieved of the unbearable burdens that have brought us to the point of suicide, to have all our financial problems solved, our relationships restored, our legal issues settled, and our tormentors punished. These are significant concerns for which we need help.

But what is most important is that we recover. And central to that recovery is a spiritual healing that provides clarity about who we are and the purpose for which we have been sent into the world. Without that healing, we remain blind to what our lives are all about. Spiritual blindness renders all solutions temporary. It will circle us back into one crisis after another.

Bartimaeus asks to receive his sight, and that healing is granted. All his other problems remain. But in this process, Bartimaeus has been given three priceless gifts in addition to his sight. The first was God's affirmation of what he had suspected all along: sometimes, we must summon the courage to trust our own inner voice when most of the world is telling us to keep quiet. The second was the knowledge that he was worth God's healing touch when all his life seemed to suggest he was not. The third was the gift of a spiritual purpose: he received his sight, *and he followed Jesus on the way."*

These three gifts, courage, self-worth, and spiritual purpose, are core to our recovery. Without them, we will wander in and out of one self-defeating attitude after another. With them, the sky is the limit.

Let us enter today's reading in the shoes of Bartimaeus. Jesus has called us. We stand before him. He asks: "What do you want me to do for you?"

Something to think about:

How do you become empowered to ask hard questions of yourself? What are your three gifts of courage, self-worth, and spiritual?

Prayer

Jesus, my life has been a pursuit of many things, some of questionable moral value but others that most would consider admirable and praiseworthy. I realize that I often have not pursued being a whole person, able to summon the courage to stand alone if need be, connected to your healing power, or engaged in a quest to find my spiritual purpose. Now, I have been brought to this point of unbearable pain. I lay aside all the pursuits of my life in order to become a whole person through your healing power. This is what I want you to do for me. Thank you for having already begun that work, which I accept by faith. Amen.

"Fear cripples us to fulfill our true potential. It's better to be fearless than worthless."-- *Nelisa Moffatt*

DAY ELEVEN

But [Elijah] himself went a day's jour-
ney into the wilderness and came and sat
down under a broom tree. And he asked
that he might die, saying, "It is enough;
now, O LORD, take away my life, for I am
no better than my fathers."-- 1 Kgs. 19:4

Elijah is traditionally regarded as the greatest Old
Testament prophet. He stood for the finest traditions of moral teaching and consistently called
those in power to acknowledge the needs of the
poor and vulnerable. He promoted a radical sense
of social justice faithful to the spirit of the covenant God made with Israel.

Though Elijah had died about 850 BC, it was
widely believed he would return to announce the
arrival of the Messiah hundreds of years later.
Many held the view that John the Baptist fulfilled
Elijah's mission in anticipation of Jesus's ministry. When Jesus needed heavenly support in the
days immediately preceding his trial and execu-

tion, it was Moses (Liberator/Lawgiver) and Elijah (Prophet extraordinaire) who met him on the Mount of Transfiguration.

Given all this, it might surprise us to learn that this renowned spiritual leader, with whom even Jesus consulted, went through a period of wishing to die. "And he asked that he might die, saying, 'it is enough; now, O Lord, take away my life...'" Were God to grant his request, God would have become the means by which Elijah killed himself. We might call this "suicide by prayer."

Suicidal thinking is no stranger to some of the most accomplished and capable people in history. The list would not only include folks in the entertainment world like Don Cornelius, Marilyn Monroe, Halle Berry, Pete Davidson, and Owen Wilson, but moral leaders as well. At one point, friends of Abraham Lincoln had to take his pocket knife away to prevent him from harming himself. The great preacher Charles Spurgeon once said, "I am the subject of depressions of spirit so fearful that I hope none of you ever get to such extremes of wretchedness as I go to." Spiritual author Eckhart Tolle describes waking up in the middle of the night suffering from unbearable dread and thoughts of suicide.

What is God's message to us through these persons? Going through a period of suicidal thinking is not a measure of our worth. Nor is it a gauge of God's love for us or our spiritual maturity. Some of the most loving, gifted people I know have fallen under this shadow.

In contrast to the shame and stigma imposed by society, it is not an indication that we are sick, sinful, selfish, or stupid. What suicidal thinking almost always signifies is that we are going through a season of unbearable pain. In a paraphrase of Elijah's feelings, "I've had enough!"

While those who die by suicide each year number in the thousands, those who recover from suicidal thinking number in the millions. This leaves us without excuse. If Elijah, with God's help, could find spiritual strength, not only to resist the impulse to die but to rediscover the purpose of his life, surely, we can as well.

Something to think about:

What are some of your spiritual strengths? Are there others that would be more helpful and others that would be less?

Prayer

God of Truth, I confess my tendency to mentally check out of this recovery process by succumbing to any number of questionable beliefs: that I am too damaged or too lost, that I have made too many mistakes or have been on the wrong path for too long, that my life is too complicated or too settled, that my pain is too deep or too insignificant. I accept this one truth, O Lord. My life matters to you. By your grace, help my life matter as much to me and respond to your offer of healing. Amen.

"Out of suffering have emerged the strongest souls; the most massive characters are seamed with scars." -- *LH. Chapin*

DAY TWELVE

Then Jezebel sent a messenger to Elijah, saying, "So may the gods do to me and more also, if I do not make your life as the life of one of them [kill you] by this time tomorrow."

[Elijah said] "For the people of Israel have forsaken your covenant, thrown down your altars, and killed your prophets with the sword, and I, even I only, am left, and they seek my life, to take it away."

-- 1 Kgs. 19:2,14

In today's reading, Jezebel pronounces a 24-hour death sentence upon Elijah. This is not simply a threat. She has the power to carry it out. It is this real stressor that has prompted Elijah to ask God to kill him. If he is going to die anyway, he wants it to be on his own terms.

Let's be clear. If the circumstances of your life have brought you to the point of considering suicide, something real and devastating is generally happening to you. As I have already written, you cannot begin to recover until you can name those unbearable circumstances.

As part of that first stage of recovery, having someone acknowledge those unbearable circumstances and validate your feelings of desperation is essential. Run from anyone who tries to reduce what you are going through to a simple misunderstanding or who minimizes what you are experiencing.

One of the major factors in my suicidal thinking at the time of my divorce was feeling trapped by the legal system. In an agonized session with my therapist, I blurted out, "I feel like the legal system is crazy."

She simply said, "That's because it is." Her validation was all it took to bring me back to hopefulness.

Complete this sentence: "I feel that _____ is killing me."

My simple response to you? That's because it is.

In that sense, Elijah gets it right. Jezebel is killing him or trying to. In another sense, Elijah gets it totally wrong. He thinks that he is all alone with no one to stand with him: "I, even I only, am left." He has developed a kind of mental nearsightedness. He simply can't see the larger picture.

So God, like a spiritual optometrist, steps in to give him a corrective lens. He says to Elijah, "...I have reserved seven thousand in Israel—all whose knees have not bowed to Baal and whose mouths have not kissed him."

How could Elijah get it so wrong? How could he miss seven thousand people who were there for him? Because *stress makes a mess* of our thinking. When we are under extreme stress our minds can begin playing tricks on us by putting a 'spin' on the events we see and attaching a not-so-objective interpretation to how we perceive reality. Like Elijah, we develop a mental nearsightedness.

How does this nearsightedness show up for those of us in recovery? As an underestimate of our resources. In my personal experience, and from the stories of others recovering from suicidal thinking, it is almost always the case that we underestimate the resources that are available to us. For a list of resources that people often overlook, scan through **Appendix A: Where to Turn for Help and Support.**

But even before you do that, take a few moments for this exercise: Make a sincere prayer to God to open your mind as God opened the mind of Elijah. With God's help, ponder this: You are obviously alive today. What resources have helped you stay alive to this point?

In that list, added to the list in Appendix A, God may be giving you an Elijah moment. You are not alone.

As a person who went through a very dark period of suicidal thinking, I want to validate whatever unbearable circumstance you may be suffering.

That circumstance is real, and *many* other persons going through that same experience would also begin to consider suicide.

However, as a person who went through a very dark period of suicidal thinking, I not only want to say that you are not alone, I need to add that you are without excuse. God is giving you the gift of an Elijah moment. Make a connection to the resources you need or need more of. Do it today.

Something to think about:

Have you underestimated the resources that are available to you? What resources have helped you stay alive to this point?

Prayer

Lord of my Days, as I look at the challenges in my life, I can't see a solution. But am I like Elijah? Are there possibilities I cannot imagine? Has my stress-soaked mind become so narrowly focused that all I can see is pain and dead ends? Lord, I give myself to you. Open my mind. Help me to see your way forward by doing your will, not mine. Amen.

DAY THIRTEEN

When the people saw that Moses delayed to come down from the mountain, the people gathered themselves together to Aaron and said to him, "Up, make us gods who shall go before us. As for this Moses, the man who brought us up out of the land of Egypt, we do not know what has become of him." So Aaron said to them, "Take off the rings of gold that are in the ears of your wives, your sons, and your daughters, and bring them to me." So all the people took off the rings of gold that were in their ears and brought them to Aaron. And he received the gold from their hand and fashioned it with a graving tool and made a golden calf. And they said, "These are your gods, O Israel, who brought you up out of the land of Egypt!" And the people sat down to eat and drink and rose up to play.

-- Ex. 32:1-4, 6

In today's reading we observe the children of Israel create and form a relationship with a golden calf. It sounds strange to say, but this relationship offers a number of benefits. It is visible, tangible; its rich, golden gleam is energizing. We have experienced this, have we not? Think of the short-term shot of positive energy when we acquire something material, a piece of jewelry, a more expensive car, a shiny new appliance.

It's reassuring. The children of Israel are experiencing anxiety born out of impatience that Moses has been delayed. The presence of this golden calf temporarily relieved their anxiety. Moses might never return from his retreat, and when he does, he might leave again. But the golden calf is with them always.

It also provided them a degree of emotional freedom. Anxiety paralyzes us; it can leave us unable to move, speak, or think. It sucks all the enjoyment out of life. The golden calf sets them free. No longer riddled with anxiety, they "sat down to eat and drink and rose up to play."

Over time, we can develop a similar relationship with suicidal thinking, a kind of internal golden calf. Like God, suicidal thinking knows and understands you like few others. It "gets" the depth of your pain. It's like a friend who will always be there for you. When life becomes unbearable, you can always bring it to mind.

Your relationship with suicidal thinking gives you power and control. The world holds so many of the reins. It has the capacity to take nearly anything away: your job, your relationships, your reputation, your comfort. But it can't take this choice away, and it ultimately can't make you stay alive if you choose not to.

Because suicidal thinking is often a coping mechanism, it provides a way of dealing with anxiety: "If things become too difficult, I can always kill myself." As a result of this pressure-relief value, there is a kind of emotional freedom. People who exhibit exhilaration after a long season of depression have often discovered that their positive energy is the result of a clear, unambiguous decision to kill themselves.

Presence, power, and relief. We might call it a suicidal spirituality. I don't turn my fears over to God. I turn them over to suicidal thinking.

The love of God is freely given, but false gods are always expensive. To make the golden calf required the gold, not only of the men, not only of their wives, but also their sons and their daughters.

Engaged long-term, suicidal thinking will pick your pocket of everything precious to you: your health, your relationships, your career, your very soul. And, tragically, should it ever find expression in your life through self-injury, the lives of your sons and daughters may be taken as well. It is for our own health and well-being that the very first of the Ten Commandments reads: "I am the LORD your God, who brought you out of the land of Egypt, out of the house of slavery. You shall have no other gods before me..."

It is impossible to write about suicide without touching on the deepest issues of life, including our life with God. Healing requires the slow, steady process of developing an authentic spirituality that nourishes the Soul and replaces the counterfeit suicidal spirituality that has taken root with a vital relationship with the living God.

Every experience in life contains a truth and a lie. Suicidal thinking reveals a profound truth: we are all in search of a deep spiritual connection. Suicidal thinking also contains a pernicious lie, that we can hold it secretly within our minds without it corroding what is most important to us.

Something to think about:

What are some of your spiritual false gods? How can they be so expensive in our lives? How can I find a deep spiritual connection out of circumstances?

Prayer

Jesus, you taught that the greatest commandment was to love God with all our heart, soul, mind, and strength. Shine your light within those very depths to help us identify anything we have used to displace you. We now turn to you alone to find peace, power, understanding, and freedom. We pray that you will preserve and protect all that is precious. Help us to recover, in time, all the gold we have unwittingly thrown away. Amen.

DAY FOURTEEN

...that you, being rooted and grounded in love, may have the power to comprehend with all the saints what is the breadth and length and height and depth, and to know the love of Christ that surpasses knowledge, that you may be filled with all the fullness of God.

-- Eph. 3:17-19

I cited Carl Jung earlier in stating that the craving for alcohol was the equivalent of the spiritual thirst for wholeness, the legitimate quest for a spiritual connection gone awry. That insight became the basis for Alcoholics Anonymous, through which millions have been delivered from the self-destructive impacts of alcohol addiction.

Suicidal thinking is also a spiritual thirst for wholeness. This sounds contradictory. After all, many would say that suicidal thinking is focused on dying. Actually, this is a myth. Persons who are suicidal generally don't want to die. They don't know how to live with their pain. They are engaged in a search for peace. Some are yearning for a reconnection with loved ones who have gone before them. Some want to feel the release that comes from putting the past behind them. Others simply want rest.

Suicidal thinking, in ways similar to an addiction, is generally a sign that the spiritual understanding that has brought us to this point is not sufficient to take us forward. It is like traveling by car westward from the East Coast. Eventually, we get to the Pacific Ocean, where a car will not take us further. We need a boat.

Today's reading speaks about finding "the power to comprehend what is the breadth and length and height and depth...[of] the love of Christ that surpasses knowledge." The word for knowledge leans toward meanings like doctrine, information, or concept.

In the spiritual realm, there is absolutely no power in simply knowing a doctrine or concept. Ideas will not save us from something as tenacious as suicidal thinking. Today we have millions of religious people who *know* about forgiveness but don't feel forgiven. Who *know* about God's love, but don't feel loved. Who *know* about prayer, but don't experience a spiritual connection. Who *know* about God's will for their lives, but have no idea how to discern or follow it.

Real power, according to our text, comes to us when we can *comprehend* these things. The word in Greek literally means "to seize forcefully." When we commit ourselves to a new level to seize forcefully the truth of God's love, forgiveness, strength, and plan for our lives, we are suddenly connected to the true power source of our faith. We begin to actually experience what we believe rather than simply recite ideas.

We realize that our quest for peace, love, and freedom is the right journey, but suicide is not the right road.

Something to think about:

What are ways you experience God's love, forgiveness, grace, and spiritual connectedness? In the past and today?

Prayer

Loving God, I do indeed find myself thirsting for peace in my life, the opportunity for a fresh start, to feel total acceptance, a rest from the burdens of living, and a connection to people I love who are no longer in this world. Give me the power to seize the truths of my faith forcefully so that ideas might become convictions; convictions might become devotions of the heart, and devotions of the heart might become the energies necessary for creating a life truly worth living. Amen.

DAY FIFTEEN

But since we belong to the day, let us be sober, and put on the breastplate of faith and love, and for a helmet the hope of salvation.

-- 1 Thess. 5:8

In today's culture, we tend to think of "sober" as meaning "free of intoxication." However, the word is never used that way in the New Testament. Instead, sobriety means having a calm spirit, a clear mind, and a loving heart. This is how the word "sobriety" is used in this book. We might call it *spiritual sobriety.*

Using this definition, it is likely that many of us are struggling to stay spiritually sober. Instead of having a calm spirit, we may feel overwhelmed and agitated. Our anxious feelings build up one on top of another until we are either paralyzed, unable to move, or set about in a frenzy, unable to stop. Because we focus on what is beyond our control and neglect what is within our control, we risk losing *all* control. This is the very opposite of faith in God.

Instead of having a clear mind, we are beset with confused, runaway, "sticky thinking." We get stuck in repeated cycles of negative thinking that dwell on experiences from the past or imagined experiences in the future. We jump back and forth between thoughts about our perceived failures to thoughts about the failures of others who have harmed us in some way.

In contrast to the urgings of the Bible to think about "whatever is true, whatever is honorable, whatever is just, whatever is pure, whatever is lovely, whatever is commendable [or]...worthy of praise," our sticky thinking keeps coming back to focus on what is ugly and wrong. It is difficult to pry these sticky thoughts off the better thoughts we want to have.

Our reading speaks of the importance of protecting the head from this vulnerability with a helmet that is "the hope of salvation." Maintaining a positive, hopeful attitude that we *can* recover and protecting our mind from invasive, negative thoughts is critical to our sobriety.

Finally, instead of having a loving heart, our capacity to love shrinks like a plant choked by all the weeds crowding in on it. It becomes difficult to love ourselves and others; we are left wondering if we are capable of love or worth being loved by anyone, even God. It is significant that our reading speaks of putting on "the breastplate of faith."

A breastplate is a piece of armor that protects the heart. Protecting the heart so that it can continue to give and receive love is key to creating a life worth living.

By the time we have begun thinking about suicide, we may have been out of spiritual sobriety so long that we have developed a tolerance for our agitation, racing thoughts, and love-starved hearts. It feels so normal and inevitable that it can be difficult to muster the motivation to regain our calm spirits, clear thinking, and loving hearts. How do we change that?

Many of us have learned that it is impossible to command ourselves to stop thinking about suicide because the command itself requires that we think about suicide! What we can do is focus on our spiritual sobriety. If we work on developing a calm spirit, a clear mind, and a loving heart, much of our suicidal thinking will begin to take care of itself.

This is a process that requires effort, an openness of heart, and a willingness to consider new perspectives. We don't have to be perfect; we will fall off the wagon many times. Forgiving ourselves, and recommitting to our recovery is what counts.

As our friends in every addiction recovery group have learned, attaining and maintaining our spiritual sobriety requires reliance on a Spiritual Source, which we affirm is the beginning of healing and vital living.

Every day, we are invited to begin anew by placing our lives into God's loving hands.

Something to think about:

What is your definition of spiritual sobriety? What does your breastplate of hope and love and your helmet of hope look like?

Prayer

God, when I think about the state of my thinking and feeling, I realize that much of my life has become unmanageable. I have tried to handle this on my own, but I only find myself going over the same small circle of thinking again and again. I need your help in prying the negative thoughts off from the positive thoughts I want to have. I turn myself over to you in faith, with hope, and trusting your love. Amen.

DAY SIXTEEN

And Samson said to the young man who held him by the hand, "Let me feel the pillars on which the house rests, that I may lean against them." Now the house was full of men and women. All the lords of the Philistines were there, and on the roof there were about 3,000 men and women, who looked on while Samson entertained. And Samson grasped the two middle pillars on which the house rested, and he leaned his weight against them, his right hand on the one and his left hand on the other. And Samson said, "Let me die with the Philistines."

-- Judg. 16:26-27, 29-30

"When a deep injury is done to us, we never recover until we forgive." -- *Alan Paton*

We have mentioned two of the several motivations that can drive someone to consider suicide:

The need to escape and the need to control. Today's reading gives us insight into a third: the need to punish. Sometimes, it is the injustice of being harmed by those who seem to be getting away with it that is the unbearable circumstance in our lives.

If anyone might feel justified in taking revenge, it would be Samson. Betrayed by the woman he loves and imprisoned by the Philistines who gouge out his eyes, he has lost all control over his own life. He has one option left: suicide. In that suicide, he will not only get revenge on the men who have tortured him; he will kill thousands of other men and women as well.

Through this passage, God invites us into a searching self-examination, one that is essential to our recovery. We must summon all the courage and honesty we can as we ponder these questions:

1. Invite the Spirit of God to bring to mind the names of those who have wronged you. Be specific. What have they done that has been so painful?

2. In your imagination, how might you hope the news of your potential suicide might impact them? Will they be shocked? Will they be overcome with guilt? Will they be sorry?

3. Think of the people who have not actively harmed you but have passively stood by and allowed others to harm you without accountability. What are their names? How would you want them to feel if you died by suicide?

4. Finally, think of those who refuse to understand how much pain you are in and have left you isolated in your suffering. Again, what are their names? How would you want them to feel if you died by suicide?

There is a reason the word "forgive" is found in over 200 verses of the Bible. Forgiveness is essential to our own well-being. "Not forgiving," writes Anne Lamott, "is like drinking rat poison and expecting the rat to die." No instance of this is more true than in revenge by suicide. We are the ones who will die by our lack of forgiveness.

Forgiveness is the only antidote that will drain this poison from our lives. You may not be ready to forgive every name on your list. Perhaps you can forgive one person today and work on the rest of the list in the days ahead.

Forgiveness does not change the past, but without forgiveness, we have no future. Ancient spiritual teachers like Jesus and modern researchers agree on this point: forgiveness makes us healthier, happier, and stronger. And it doesn't cost a nickel.

Something to think about:

What are ways you forgive others? Do you forgive yourself when God has forgiven you?

Prayer

Merciful God, I confess the ways that I have held unforgiveness in my heart. I now realize that I have taken a poison into my soul that is threatening my very life. Hear me as I name before you, [and perhaps one other person], those that I now forgive. I release them from the penalties I have imagined that my suicide would visit upon their lives. Flood my inner being with your healing and loving kindness as I pray for your blessing upon them, one by one. Amen.

DAY SEVENTEEN

The Spirit of the Lord is upon me, because he has anointed me to proclaim good news to the poor. He has sent me to proclaim liberty to the captives and recovering of sight to the blind, to set at liberty those who are oppressed...

-- Luke 4:18

This was to fulfill what was spoken by the prophet Isaiah: "He took our infirmities and bore our diseases."

-- Matt. 8:17 (NIV)

When we think of the healing ministry of Jesus, we usually focus on the physical. We picture people throwing aside crutches and rising out of wheelchairs, the instant remission of cancer, or the recovery of sight. In fact, the Greek word for "disease" always refers to a physical illness in the Bible. Miracles still happen.

But the Greek word for "infirmity" is used with many other meanings in the New Testament. In particular, the Apostle Paul almost always uses the word to speak of a weakness, sometimes emotional weakness, sometimes a weakness of will, sometimes a moral weakness, other times weakness in the face of overpowering circumstances that one cannot control or endure.

In addition, the "oppressed" that Jesus refers to as the focus of his public ministry could be further described as those who are bruised, broken, and downtrodden. All this suggests that the healing ministry of Jesus not only focused on those who were physically ill but on those who were in a weakened emotional state, people who were *crushed by tragedy*.

Can we picture Jesus healing people crushed by tragedy? Can we imagine a line of people waiting for Jesus's healing whose wounds are invisible, whose crutches, canes, and wheelchairs are all inside, propping up their limping spirits, whose eyes could see twenty-twenty were it not for the tears that filled them and spilled down their faces? Do we think it possible that they might emerge from that encounter with relief from the unbearable ache of a shattered heart, with the restoration of an unassailable dignity that had been stolen by multiple rejections, with a resurgence of purpose in a life once deemed meaningless, with love pouring from enlarged souls that had once been only a collection of shards held together by the thin wires of a weakened will?

Faith begins with an inspired imagination. Jesus promised, "You will say to this mountain, 'Move from here to there,' and it will move..." But the starting point of faith is not the mountain; it is the capacity to *imagine the mountain moving.*

Today's reading invites us to imagine ourselves in that line of those expectantly waiting for healing. We are those who have been crushed by tragedy, upon whose shoulders have fallen some unbearable burden. But the same desperation that could drive us toward death is now leading us to seek spiritual healing. While our inclination to suicide is understandable, a small inner voice tells us this is not our destiny.

We need to stand in this line and exercise faith. Faith is not "doing nothing." Faith is actively engaging the imagination to envision the inner healing we need. We will only receive what we can imagine.

And so, there are three groups in the ministry of Jesus, always three groups. There are those waiting expectantly for healing, who can imagine something better. Then, there are those who are experiencing that healing touch. And, finally, there are those watching from a place of safety but spiritually sterile distance.

Something to think about:

Which group are we in, and why is there something we need to learn from this?

Prayer

Healing Spirit, assist me by your grace to imagine a scene new to my thinking, the healing of sadness, broken-heartedness, despair, self-sabotage and self-deprecation, anxiety-ridden dreams, and catastrophic thinking. Remove the inner crutch of suicidal thinking from my soul that keeps me from putting my full weight upon you, that doubts your healing power, and prevents me from finding rest. I now move from the crowd of those watching to the line of those waiting, imagining a day when I will be walking, head high and heart whole. Amen.

DAY EIGHTEEN

*For to the one who has, more will be given,
and from the one who has not, even what
he has will be taken away.*

-- Mark 4:25

For a number of years, I found this passage incomprehensible. What kind of God takes from a person what little they have and gives it to someone who has more than enough? The whole of the Bible rails against this kind of treatment of the impoverished. Then, I came to realize that the source of my confusion was a focus on the material rather than the attitudinal. What Jesus is addressing here are the dangers of a scarcity mindset.

I define a scarcity mindset as an obsessive focus on what one does not have. If I have a dollar, a scarcity mindset focuses on the dollar I don't have. It focuses on the house I don't have, the car, the friends, the job, the love I don't have, and on and on.

A scarcity mentality also sees the world as a fixed pie. If someone has more, it automatically means I have less. A scarcity mentality positions me in a perpetual state of jealousy and competition. There is no faster way to poison, and then lose relationships than adopting a scarcity mentality.

A scarcity mentality causes you to lose other things as well—like the ability to think. Having a scarcity mentality can lower your IQ by as many as 14 points.[3] It dumbs you down.

A scarcity mentality makes you less valuable as an employee. It affects your ability to solve problems, hold information, and reason logically. It also affects your brain's decision-making process. It limits your ability to plan, focus, and start a project or task. Your brain is too busy thinking about something you don't have.

So, as Jesus observed, a scarcity mentality causes you to lose one thing after another until, eventually, you lose even the little you have.

In any recovery process, including this one, the initial progress is always going to be small. After months of wanting to die, I still remember a single July morning when I felt like living. It was only a single morning. Compared to an entire week, it was nothing. A scarcity mentality would have focused on all the other dark days. Somehow, by the grace of God, I dropped down to my knees and gave thanks.

---

3   https://www.webmd.com/mental-health/what-is-scarcity-mentality

This, then, is the antidote to a scarcity mindset: an attitude of gratitude. The science is clear. Gratitude improves mental health, supports heart health, improves sleep, lessens depression...it just makes us happier. It leads to better interpersonal relationships, helps us develop stronger bonds with others and builds a sense of community.

Notice the pattern. While a scarcity mentality keeps subtracting—relationships, intelligence, productivity, an attitude of gratitude keeps adding—happiness, health, relationships. To the one who has, more is given, and from the one who has not, even what they have is taken away.

I have now witnessed the recovery process of hundreds of persons over the course of my lifetime. The difference between those who experience healing and those who do not often comes down to this. Those who recover begin to be grateful for the small improvements they experience, and that begins to build. They keep growing like a snowball rolling down a hillside.

The entire sky may be cloudy at first, except for one small patch of blue. But that small patch of blue is where they focus their attention because they know there is a lot more blue sky above the clouds than there are clouds hiding the blue sky.

Something to think about:

What are the things you do to praise God when you have a smile in your heart? How do you celebrate? What kind of spiritual practice could you implement to grow in gratitude?

Prayer

Generous God, show me the ways that my mind perceives scarcity and simply reproduces more scarcity. Reveal to me the gifts, large and small, that are coming to me in this recovery process. Help me recognize those gifts of growth, even if they are small, to receive them as seeds planted in my soul, which will grow into greater health and strength. Give me a grateful heart, for gratitude is the soil in which everything good must find its root. Amen.

DAY NINETEEN

So Elijah went and did according to the word of the LORD. He went and lived by the brook Cherith that is east of the Jordan. And the ravens brought him bread and meat in the morning, and bread and meat in the evening, and he drank from the brook.

-- 1 Kgs. 17:5-6

For you shall be in league with the stones of the field, and the beasts of the field shall be at peace with you.

-- Job 5:23

In an age dominated by chemical, technological, and pharmaceutical remedies, it is easy to forget the healing, life-giving power that can be derived from contact with the natural world. At the lowest point in his life, Elijah, teetering on the edge of death, is fed bread and meat by the ravens and hydrated by water from a brook.

In the midst of all his suffering, Job can envision being at peace with the beasts of the field. The word "peace" in our English Bibles is a translation of the Hebrew "shalom" which means to be safe, completed, friendly, whole. And when Jesus went through his wilderness temptation, we are told he was with wild animals and angels who ministered to him.

Many people find that contact with nature, either through owning a pet or being outdoors, is another rich source of meaning. Numerous studies reveal that owning a pet not only offers companionship but can also help alleviate depression, facilitate psycho-therapy, lower blood pressure, and prevent premature death from heart attacks.

Conversely, losing a beloved pet, either to death or relinquishment made necessary by incapacity, can be one of the unbearable circumstances that trigger suicidal thinking. Imagine Elijah's state of mind if the ravens had suddenly stopped visiting him. If you have lost a pet, see the resources in Appendix B: Coping with the Loss of a Pet.

In response to the tech-boom burnout, depression, and high suicide rates, the practice of forest bathing has emerged in Japan. Studies reveal that "forest bathing" (shinrin-yoku) has positive physiological effects. Spending time in forests or simply looking at pictures of trees reaps a number of benefits, such as blood pressure reduction, improvement of autonomic and immune functions, as well as the psychological effects of alleviating depression and improving mental health.

Contact with the natural world can provide an important dose of pain relief, but in order to receive that benefit, we must get beyond our biases that other creatures are soulless lifeforms or that matter is simply dead, lifeless "stuff."

During a time when my mind was jumbled with chaotic thoughts racing through my head, I remembered that there was a river nearby with tree-lined banks. Among the trees was a picnic shelter-house constructed of huge, beautiful stones. I drove there, positioned myself on the ground next to the north wall, and leaned my head against one of the stones.

I prayed:

> Brother Stone, I now open myself to the beauty of what God has created you to be. Please give the gift of stability to my mind. Let your strong, calm, steady essence flow through the flesh and bone of my body and into my mind. Restore my peace. Calm my spirit.

That's when I discovered what Job meant by being "in league with the stones of the field."

At the wrong dosages, all medicines are poisonous. The intensity of nature manifest in cataclysms of one sort or another can certainly be destructive to human life. But at the right dosage, contact with the plants and animals of God's created order can be an essential element of our recovery process. And, in this season of planetary peril, we can be an essential element of theirs.

Like all treatments, we will never know its benefits by simply thinking about it. We must take the medicine.

Something to think about:

What are some ways God connects with you in nature? Outside of your everyday norm? Does this fill your cup or not? Why?

Prayer

Healing Spirit, thank you for all the ways you are reaching out to ease my pain. I confess a degree of stubbornness that insists on healing that comes in my way and on my timetable. Once again, I set aside my will and open my heart to your will. The world that you have created lies all about me. Give me grace so that I might not neglect its healing powers, that I might take the medicine of spending time in its hospital, and that I might live with faith and positive expectation. Amen.

DAY TWENTY

Jesus replied, "A man was going down from Jerusalem to Jericho, and he fell among robbers, who stripped him and beat him and departed, leaving him half dead. Now by chance a priest was going down that road, and when he saw him he passed by on the other side...But a Samaritan, as he journeyed, came to where he was, and when he saw him, he had compassion."

--Luke 10:30-31, 33

In today's reading, a man endures a horrific experience. According to psychologist Linda Karlovec, PhD, it contains the four elements that are core to any severe trauma: (1) excruciating pain combined with (2) feeling alone, (3) confused, and (4) powerless.

He is set upon by a band of robbers who have been lying in ambush. Outnumbered, it is not enough that they should overpower him and steal his possessions. In an act of utter humiliation, they strip him bare. But even that is not enough. They savagely beat him. They leave him along the roadside, naked, presumably unconscious, half-dead, teetering between life and death.

The seemingly good news is that a priest is not far behind, which kindles hope of a rescue. The actual sad news is that the priest is of no help. He doesn't further harm the beaten man. He simply crosses the road to the other side and rides past him. Whatever the reason, he is indifferent, and if this were the end of the story, that indifference would have been maintained at the cost of the beaten man's life.

Indifference can be a killer, especially when it is the indifference of someone you would expect to care. In this case, it was a priest, but it could have just as well been other familiar faces avoiding him: work associates, faith community members, friends, and even family members.

Holocaust survivor Elie Weisel wrote, "The opposite of love is not hate; it's indifference. The opposite of art is not ugliness; it's indifference. The opposite of faith is not heresy; it's indifference. And the opposite of life is not death; it's indifference."

For those of us who have had the experience of something so unbearable that we begin to consider suicide, dealing with perceived indifference is one of the greatest challenges of the recovery process. How can someone be indifferent to our feelings of desperation? How can they not see how our life experience is crushing us?

In the struggle for survival, the temptation to internalize this indifference can be a swift current against which to swim. The silence of indifference shouts at us: Maybe you aren't worth saving.

It is often a specific person's indifference that we find so difficult to deal with. But this reading invites us to pay attention to another figure coming down the road: "But a Samaritan, as he journeyed, came to where he was, and when he saw him, he had compassion." One man's compassion shattered the smothering silence of indifference.

It is my experience that God always sends this second person down the road in one guise or another, often someone you would least expect. I had spent years working to block gay men and women from ordination to ministry. But when nearly everyone else was passing me by in my desperate state, it was a gay man who knocked on my door. He spent hours with me, helped me find a gig as a retreat leader, which put a few dollars in my pocket and introduced me to a group of people who valued what I had to offer.

The ultimate good Samaritan is God. God is never indifferent to our suffering. God always forgives, always has compassion, always accepts us. God never gives up on us, never abandons us, never considers us too much work. And God will always show up, sometimes in the face of someone you would least expect.

And so, we are the ones who find ourselves on the edge of that road, humiliated, teetering between life and death. Through our blurry eyes, there are two figures approaching us, always two. One is painfully indifferent. The other is the very essence of Divine Love.

I have waited until this day to say something so difficult to hear, but so important to speak: we will never be able to recover as long as we are waiting on those who are indifferent to break their silence. We must let go of that expectation.

We can recover as long as we remember that un-expected second person on the road, that very essence of Divine Love who is reaching to lift us up, heal us, and carry us with him.

Two persons coming down that road, always two. Where will we focus?

Indifference will kill us. Love will save us.

Something to think about:

Have you ever felt indifference in your journey? What are ways you combat this indifference?

Who are those in your life who, "Like the Priest," you are waiting for them to come and they do not?

Prayer

Good Samaritan God, I confess my tendency to push you aside in my thinking, to focus on the in-difference of a few to the neglect of the unfailing love of the One. Forgive my misplaced attention that uses disappointment as an excuse for self-pity. Open my heart to the second person you always send down the road, and open my eyes to see that they are actually you in human disguise. Give me a grateful heart for every act of love, large and small, that lifts me from this roadside of despair. Amen.

DAY TWENTY-ONE

Disgrace and confuse all who want me dead; turn away and disgrace all who want to hurt me. Embarrass and shame everyone who says, "Just look at you now!"

-- Psalm 40:14-15 (CEV)

While people of faith may feel reluctant to speak in the stark terms found in today's reading, many of us who are recovering from suicidal thinking are dealing with something even more lethal than indifference. We are trying to cope with those who are actively involved in trying to hurt us or even want us dead. The Bible is realistic on this matter, and today's reading is on point.

The unbearable situation that immediately comes to mind is bullying. Bullying is an ongoing and deliberate misuse of power in relationships through repeated verbal, physical, or social behavior that intends to cause physical, social, or psychological harm. At the school-age stage of life, bullying can interfere with normal developmental and educational processes. Twenty-five percent of 16-24-year-olds recall instances of being bullied, which doubles their suicide risk later in life.

But it also places children at an unnecessary additional risk for suicidal thoughts and actions. And it doesn't stop there. Adults who reported bullying in childhood were more than twice as likely as older adults to attempt suicide later in life.

Bullying isn't only experienced at school. Research reveals that workplace bullying is relatively common as well. It occurs in situations where a person receives repeated negative behavior, mistreatment, or abuse at work from others within the organization. Roughly 15% of workers have experienced workplace bullying in the last six months. Current and past experiences of workplace bullying were associated with an increased risk of suicidal ideation.Today's reading would also apply to victims of intimate partner violence, abuse, or aggression that occurs within a romantic relationship. Survivors of intimate partner violence are twice as likely to attempt suicide multiple times.

Parental alienation is also a means of intentionally causing great harm. Parental alienation is the anomalous, maladaptive behavior (refusal to have a relationship with a loving parent) that is driven by an abnormal emotional condition (the false belief that the rejected parent is evil, dangerous, or unworthy of love).

If you are recovering from suicidal thinking, it will be important to ask yourself several questions. Using the words of this verse:

a. Do you now, or have you ever had someone in your life who made it clear *by their behavior* that they want you dead?

b. Do you now, or have you ever had someone in your life who made it clear *by their behavior* that they wanted to intentionally hurt you?

c. Do you now, or have you ever had someone in your life who intentionally harmed you, and then rejoiced over your suffering: "Just look at you now!" (What a crybaby you are!)

These kinds of experiences can feel unbearable. Even the memory of them can stir up confusion, feelings of shame and embarrassment, and poison our self-regard to a degree that we no longer believe we are worth keeping alive. Part of the antidote to this poison is found in today's reading. Here is a paraphrase of the message:

Let's clear up your *confusion*. Whatever mistakes you have made, no one deserves to be the object of someone's *death* wish. No one deserves to be intentionally *hurt*. No one deserves to have someone harm them and then gloat over their suffering. *The person who should be ashamed, embarrassed, and disgraced is whoever inflicted this upon you.*

Getting this straight is an essential part of our recovery. What others have done to us is not our fault. But neither is it an excuse. It is time to open this wound to the disinfecting and healing light of God's truth. Let's start today.

Something to think about:

People occasionally come into our lives and want to do harm by bullying. What are some ways you can combat bullying when you encounter it?

Prayer

God of grace and truth, perhaps without knowing it, I have absorbed the poison of another's sick intentions for my life. I have been dogged by shame and embarrassment. As a result, I have thought myself less worthy of life itself. With your help, I state the truth, that whatever mistakes I have made, I have been created worthy of love and self-regard. The proper place for shame and embarrassment is on those who have wished me harm, and that is where I now place it. I refuse to allow these insults to my soul to become an excuse for half-hearted living or half-hoped for dying. Clear away all vestiges of this poison, and radiate my being with your love and light. Amen.

DAY TWENTY-TWO

*Therefore, confess your sins to one an-
other, and pray for one another, that you
may be healed.*

-- James 5:16

*If we say we have no sin, we deceive our-
selves, and the truth is not in us. If we confess our sins, he is faithful and just to forgive us our sins and to cleanse us from all
unrighteousness.*

-- 1 John 1:8-9

While a legalistic and punitive understanding of
God has made the word "sin" almost useless for
our healing process, most of us are quite aware of
them by other names: faults, mistakes, or failures.
One in five Americans lives with regret almost all
the time, and a whopping 82% of us experience
regret at least occasionally. This regret can be
weighty enough that it becomes the unbearable
circumstance that leads to suicidal thinking, es-

pecially when it contributes to our isolation or hopelessness. Even when it is a secondary factor, it can complicate our recovery process if avoided.

What are the faults/failures/mistakes that people regret the most? We tend to regret having the courage to be ourselves. I call this the sin of chicken. We tend to regret being so focused on work of one kind or another, that we have missed the joy of living and loving. We tend to regret not being more honest in expressing our true feelings, particularly toward those that we love.

We tend to regret the neglect of important relationships especially friends and loved ones we have lost touch with. Or the relationships where we have broken contact over relatively small issues. We tend to regret not letting ourselves be happier and being more grateful for the gifts in our lives. We can all think of times when we were jealous, resentful, or judgmental, as well as times when we failed to keep our promises or be our best selves.

Notice from today's reading the assumption that we all have failures that we regret. It doesn't suggest that some have sinned and others haven't. In fact, the second reading is clear: "If we say we have no sin we deceive ourselves and the truth is not in us."

How do we deal with these things?

It is an interesting paradox of the spiritual realm that naming what is broken begins to heal it. Avoiding what is broken makes it break even further. In the words of psychotherapist Carl Jung, "What we resist not only persists but will grow in size."

In the Bible, naming the faults/failures /mistakes that we regret is called confession. Confession simply means that we speak aloud what we already know inside. We do not need to adopt a sacramental perspective on confession that would require the presence of a church official. Making a list of our regrets and sharing those with another trusted human being who will pray with us can be effective as well.

Notice from this verse that we do not confess these things for God's benefit but for our own. Often, what we keep in secret makes us sick and unhealthy. We confess our sins to one another and pray for one another in order to be healed. It will be difficult for us to recover from our suicidal thinking if we are weighed down by a load of regret in our souls.

After we have been honest with God, ourselves, and another trusted person, it is vital that we accept God's forgiveness, and forgive ourselves. To be forgiven by the God of the Universe but not forgive ourselves would be to waste the grace of God, like pouring sweet honey into the dirt. A lack of self-forgiveness lies at the root of many of our problems.

This is a courageous step in the healing process and one that may take several attempts to complete. Just getting out a piece of paper to begin making a list of regrets may be all you can do at first. In that case, put the list away until a later time, and give thanks that you have been able to take the first step. When regrets begin to come to mind and weigh on your heart, it is God's way of telling you that it is time to work on your list again.

Something to think about:

Make a list of faults, failures, regrets, and mistakes. What do they mean, and how can I start the healing process around these things? How can God's grace be part of this conversation?

Prayer

God, the time has come for me to take the next step in my recovery process. As I explore the regrets in my life, help me to be honest and courageous. Guide me as I find a trusted person with whom I can share these discoveries about myself. I claim your promise that as I share my regrets, I will find healing. I accept your forgiveness, and I forgive myself. I, in turn, lift up others in prayer who are recovering, that I might be a safe person for them to share their struggles, offering only healing, compassion, and understanding. Amen.

DAY TWENTY-THREE

But God has so composed the body that
there may be no division in the body, but
that the members may have the same care
for one another. If one member suffers, all
suffer together; if one member is honored,
all rejoice together.

-- 1 Cor. 12:24-26

I've always thought of these verses as *prescriptive*, a command to love one another clothed in the garb of an extended metaphor comparing our relationships to one another with the physical body. While I continue to hold this view, I now recognize the degree to which the verses are *descriptive*. In other words, suffering with others is not simply a decision; it is a fact.

Conversely, when we suffer, others inevitably suffer, too, often in ways we are unaware of.

Once upon a time, there were some passengers on a boat. As the boat pulled away from the dock to begin its voyage, one passenger opened his bag and took out a drill. The other passengers became alarmed as he put the drill bit against the floor under his seat and began to make a hole in the bottom of the boat. The other passengers, in fear and astonishment, pleaded with him, "Stop! What are you doing?"

The man was surprised by their objections. He calmly said, "What business is it of yours? Why should you care? I'm only drilling under my own seat. I have no intention of drilling under yours." The other passengers frantically told him, "The seat might only be yours, but the water will rise up to drown us all!"

This 1500-year-old parable of Rabbi Shimon bar Yochai makes a critical point. There are no purely individual acts. Everything we do affects others.

Reporting of a celebrity's suicide appears to increase the number of suicides by 8 - 18% in the two months following the celebrity's death.[4] And it's not just celebrities. Ordinary people have a bigger impact than they realize. After a speech I gave at a suicide prevention dinner, a woman shared her story with me.

"Two years ago, I lost my oldest son to suicide. Last month, his younger brother went to his grave on his birthday and took his life. I have lost both sons to suicide. Without knowing it, my older son modeled suicide for his younger brother."

---

4   https://journals.lww.com/indianjpsychiatry/full-text/2016/58040/celebrity_suicide_and_its_effect_on_further_media.16.aspx

A suicide doubles the risk of surviving family and friends harming themselves. A wife whose husband takes his own life is five times more likely to take her own. When one person suffers, all suffer together.

We may believe that the thoughts we carry around secretly in our heads can't affect anyone. But in an edition of "All Things Considered" on NPR, Stanford psychologist Carol Dweck reported: "...it's not something you can put your finger on. We're not usually aware of how we are conveying our expectations to other people, but it's there."

She was one of several researchers who have explored all kinds of surprising effects that our thoughts can have: A mother's thoughts can affect the drinking behavior of her middle-schooler. Military trainers' expectations can literally make a soldier faster or slower. Teacher expectations can raise or lower a student's IQ score.

Spiritual traditions across the ages, psychological research, and modern physics all agree. We impact one another, even at a distance, especially those with whom we are emotionally connected. When we summon our courage, we spark courage in the hearts of others. When we cultivate positive thinking, it becomes easier for others to be positive as well. When we achieve spiritual sobriety— calm spirits, clear minds, and loving hearts—others may become calmer, clearer, and more loving.

The world darkens with every act of despair. Each step we take in our recovery process makes the world a little bit brighter.

Something to think about:

Being a part of a larger community and how they interact with me, how can you be a positive influence on the people around you?

Prayer

Loving God, you have created a universe of connections where butterfly wings change the course of great storms, atoms remain entangled light-years from one another, and human spirits feel the joys and sorrows of other human spirits without a word spoken. Help me, O Lord, not only feel the weight of my responsibility for others but also the possibility that my life choices can raise the positive potential in the lives of those to whom I am forever connected. Gradually shape my thinking into a field of energy through which others walk and feel lighter without ever knowing why. Amen.

DAY TWENTY-FOUR

And when Jesus had stepped out of the boat, immediately there met him out of the tombs a man with an unclean spirit. He lived among the tombs. And no one could bind him anymore, not even with a chain, for he had often been bound with shackles and chains, but he wrenched the chains apart, and he broke the shackles in pieces. No one had the strength to subdue him. Night and day among the tombs and on the mountains he was always crying out and cutting himself with stones.

-- Mark 5:2-5

...[Jesus] went about doing good and healing all who were oppressed by the devil, for God was with him.

-- Acts 10:38

People today typically equate the demonic with evil personalities, folks like Caligula, Genghis

Kahn, Hitler, Pol Pot, or others responsible for the deaths of millions of innocent men, women, and children. However, the New Testament never speaks of individuals like Herod, Caiaphas, or Pilate as being overtaken by the devil. In the New Testament, people who are oppressed by the devil generally don't directly harm other people; they harm themselves.

We see this in today's reading. Nowhere is the man described as dangerous to others. He is dangerous to *himself*, day and night, cutting himself with stones and crying out in pain. When the force that was oppressing him was cast into a herd of swine, the herd didn't attack the persons nearby; they destroyed themselves. They rush headlong over a cliff to drown themselves in the sea.

Peter summarizes the ministry of Jesus as "doing good and healing all who were oppressed by the devil." The word oppressed is the same word used to describe Pharoah's enslavement of Israel in the Old Testament. Under his rule, the lives of the Israelites were reduced to forced labor. It is important to note that Pharoah took this action not because the Israelites were weak but because he feared their strength: "Behold, the people of Israel are too strong and too mighty for us."

If we combine the idea of enslavement with the previous concept of self-destruction, we might say this: There is a spiritual force in the universe that is seeking to enslave us through a pattern of self-destructive thinking and acting. To avoid the trap of distorted concepts like the devil, Satan, demons, demonic, and possession that we have grown up with, let us simply call this the "Dark Force."

We know that we are being oppressed by the Dark Force when we hear ourselves saying things like, "I *can't* stop thinking about my mistakes, failures, missed opportunities, losses of the past, physical imperfections, disabilities, unfair treatment, [fill in the blank]   ."

Like Pharoah, the Dark Force doesn't oppress us because we are weak or defective. Remember that Jesus himself encountered this Dark Force in the wilderness near the beginning of his ministry. It was precisely Jesus's great potential that this Force was trying to blunt.

The quote from *The Usual Suspects* comes to mind: "The greatest trick the Devil [Dark Force] ever pulled was convincing the world he didn't exist." The second greatest trick of the Dark Force was convincing us that we should play small in the world.

As Marianne Williamson wrote: "You are a child of God. Your playing small does not serve the world."

Something to think about:

Reflect on what you read. How does what I read push me to think differently about who I am in this world and how I see myself?

Prayer

Lord Jesus, I now recognize that the source of my powerlessness against certain patterns of thinking and behaving is the work of the Dark Force that is seeking to thwart the potential of my life for good in the world. I thank you for coming to heal all of us who are held hostage by this Dark Force. I now take my stand at your side and forcefully lay hold of this promise that by the power of your Spirit, I am being set free. I also choose, by your grace, to stop playing small in the world and to claim my birthright as a child of God. And I will pray this prayer as often as I must until every link of these oppressive chains is broken in my life. Amen.

DAY TWENTY-FIVE

Resist the devil, and he will flee from you.

-- James 4:7

The research facility in Oracle, Arizona, known as Biosphere 2, is essentially a giant terrarium with perfect conditions for growing anything. Researchers discovered that trees grown indoors with perfect amounts of sunlight and water in perfect soil never mature. After a period of rapid vertical growth, they simply fall over. It turns out that without the occasional buffeting of the wind, trees never develop the "stress wood" that makes their trunks strong enough and their roots deep enough to support their height. Trees need something to resist, in this case, the wind, in order to develop.

This is true for human beings as well. Without resisting the pull of gravity, our bodies would never develop the muscle and bones that are necessary for human health. The bodies of astronauts in zero gravity begin to deteriorate quickly unless some resistance training is introduced to replace the downward pull that we on Earth must contend with every day. Resistance is essential to our existence.

Resistance is also essential to creativity. A stream that runs unimpeded to the ocean is featureless. It runs in a straight line. But place a stone in the middle to obstruct its flow, and whirlpools will be created all around it. Add a few more stones, and the stream creates a waterfall. Add even more, and the stream begins to carve out intricate patterns in the clay of its banks as it creates more complex ways of reaching its destination. The Grand Canyon would not have achieved its majestic beauty if the Colorado River that carved it ran straight to the Pacific Ocean without any obstacles. It would simply be a Grand Ditch.

Today's reading urges us to "resist the devil." At first, it seems odd that God would permit a Dark Force to exist that we must resist. There are no easy answers to the presence of evil in the world, but this much is certain. Without the obstacles thrown in the path of human beings in general, and individuals in particular, there would be no great works of art, no soaring symphonies, no enthralling books of fiction or riveting movies, no life-altering scientific discoveries, no technological wonders, no heroic deeds of loyalty and love in the face of seemingly impossible odds.

This book of several hundred pages essentially outlines a spiritual project designed to resist the various roots of suicidal thinking, with the ultimate goal of freeing us from its hold over our inner life altogether. Why is such resistance required of us? Because without it, we will never develop into the magnificent spiritual beings we were sent into the world to become.

Resist the devil and he will flee from you. We don't have to defeat the devil. We don't have to eliminate all the obstacles to human happiness in the world. What we must do is *resist*. Put up a fight.

We must *resist* the "stinking thinking" that we are alone, worthless, and irredeemable.

We must *resist* the notion that our lives are meaningless, that the world would be better off without us, and that we have no purpose to fulfill on earth.

We must *resist* the temptation to believe that God has abandoned us, desires to punish us, or that a vital relationship with God is possible for others but not for us.

We must *resist* the idea that we can keep living the same way but have a different outcome.

If we resist the devil, he will flee from us. It is through the process of resisting that we grow into the magnificent spiritual beings that we were born to become.

If we do not resist the devil, he will run *toward* us. That is simply another way of saying that negativity begins to attract more negativity. All the religious services of a lifetime cannot save a person from that.

Something to think about:

Sometimes it simply comes down to resistance. Pushing back against. How are ways you resist feeling of feeling abandonment, evil, and meaningless? Who in your life is there to help with you need this resistance?

Prayer

Loving God, how easy it is for me to see the challenges thrown against me as insurmountable obstacles to my happiness. I confess the many times that I have simply given in to defeat rather than creatively resisted the various temptations to despair. I have failed to resist, to put up a fight for better health, better thinking, better decisions, and a better life. I now call upon the power of your Holy Spirit to renew my resolve against all that would harm me and those that I love. I trust that resisting the Dark Force is an act of faith that you honor and uphold. Amen.

DAY TWENTY-SIX

He was a murderer from the beginning, and does not stand in the truth, because there is no truth in him. When he lies, he speaks out of his own character, for he is a liar and the father of lies.

-- John 8:44

So Jesus said to the Jews who had believed him, "If you abide in my word, you are truly my disciples, and you will know the truth, and the truth will set you free."

-- John 8:31-32

Sometimes, the source of our unbearable pain is found in our own thinking.

A number of years ago, a young man I shall call Don was sitting in my office. He had been raised in the upscale community where the church was located. Now, in his late twenties and working a blue-collar job, he realized he would never be able to afford a home in the community he had grown up in. He internalized this as failure and defectiveness. In fact, his belief went straight to his identity: "If I can never purchase a home in this community, I am a total failure, and I don't know how to live with that."

And he didn't. Don took his life a few weeks later.

There were many factors, but from a spiritual standpoint, it came down to this: Don had been killed by a lie. The community we live in does not make us a success or failure. Success is a matter of the heart, "for everyone who loves is born of God and knows God," as John writes. No one who is born of God and knows God is a failure.

In today's reading, Jesus is teaching about the devil, the Dark Force, the one we are called to resist. Jesus doesn't mince words. This Dark Force is a murderer. But it doesn't kill people by throwing them out windows or attacking them with flying objects. It brings people to the point of self-destructing by getting them to believe things that are not true.

And this Dark Force is good at it. We are twice as likely to kill ourselves than be killed by another person. But our thinking can do a lot of damage short of physical self-injury. The average person has 40,000 negative thoughts each day. Even the most confident individuals fall prey to negative, judgmental, irrational, fear-based thoughts that erode the abundant life that Jesus promised.

What makes these lies so difficult to deal with is that they feel true. They may feel true because we have been told them from our childhood. They may feel true because the messages from society keep reinforcing them. They may feel true simply because we have made a habit of allowing everything that pops into our heads to go unchallenged. This results in a kind of bondage, an addiction to negativity.

To Don, the belief that he was a failure, reinforced by what he had heard from the time he was a child, the toxic arrogance of the community he grew up in, and his undeveloped spiritual muscles made it difficult for him to shake off his negative thinking as a lie. It felt oh so true to him.

Jesus promised "you will know the truth and the truth will set you free." The word "know" in this verse means much more than intellectual assent. It is the same word used for sexual intimacy between a man and a woman. The truth that sets us free is the one we take deep into our souls, study, meditate upon, and memorize. Jesus says we can find this truth by abiding, dwelling in, his words.

In Appendix B, you will find a fifteen-day exercise that takes Jesus at his word. Each day, there is a thought based on a saying from Jesus. Take three minutes to repeat that out loud. Then, memorize the Scripture it is based on.

If we think what we always thought, we will feel what we have always felt, and we will do what we have always done.

Something to think about:

What lies are you currently telling yourself? What practical ways can you start to combat this thinking? If you take up the challenge, what did you find helpful or encouraging?

Prayer

Lord of truth, my mind is awash with many negative thoughts, some of which I have thought for so long that they feel normal. Reveal to me the ones that are being used by the Dark Force to my detriment. Help me to dwell in your words of life so that the prison bars of my own thinking might be burst asunder, and I might be set free at last. Amen.

DAY TWENTY-SEVEN

Then the devil took him...to the highest point of the Temple, and said, "If you are the Son of God, jump off"...Jesus responded, "The Scriptures also say, 'You must not test the Lord your God.'"

-- Luke 4:9,12 (NLT)

Let the word of Christ dwell in you richly, teaching and admonishing one another in all wisdom, singing psalms and hymns and spiritual songs, with thankfulness in your hearts to God.

-- Col. 3:16

Jesus never answered a single temptation with the word "No." He undoubtedly realized that it is impossible for a person to tell themselves not to think a particular thought. The process of not thinking something necessarily begins by thinking it, and then telling yourself not to, over and over again!

Jesus responds to every temptation, including the one in today's reading, with an alternative thought designed to replace the temptation.

This is a Biblical principle: to experience inner healing we must replace soul-corroding thoughts with the truth of God, what I call a sacred thought-swap. Since most of us have grown accustomed to living with some of the most soul-corrosive thinking imaginable, and over many decades, learning how to do this thought-swap that Jesus modelled is new.

The first step is recognizing that many things we do to find relief are temporary if they do not change our thinking. Eating at a fine restaurant (dollars turned to bread), listening to our favorite music, watching an inspiring show, or taking a trip can be wonderful...and recommended...but if these do not change our soul-corrosive thinking, we simply snap back into our erratic moods.

The second step is establishing a standard for evaluating a thought. If our standard is (a) seniority – how many years I have had the thought, (b) immediacy – what is the first thought that comes to mind, or (c) familiarity – does this thought *feel* familiar, then just about any thought will do. If, on the other hand, God alone is the standard of truth, then thoughts must be held up against the yardstick of God's Word.

The third step is identifying specific thoughts that need to be swapped out. For example, it is easy to have the thought: "I am a defective person because things feel unbearable in my life." That thought is corrosive to the soul and is living rent-free in our mental space. But it also can't be right. Some of the most spiritual persons who have ever lived have struggled with thoughts of suicide. The Bible declares that "we are God's *masterpiece.*" (Eph. 2:10) So, the truth is that "I am God's masterpiece."

The fourth step is to pray a prayer that evicts the old thought and replaces it with the new one. Since we are spiritual beings, it is not enough to just say it. We must also pray it. Praying a thought shifts the spiritual ground on which we stand.

The fifth step is to nourish the new thought, to let it dwell in us *richly.* To dwell means to take up permanent residence. To dwell richly means to give the thought the honor it is due. It does us little good to take in a thought from Christ if we then treat it like a pauper and keep it hidden away in a back room.

Admonishing one another in all wisdom means giving people who love us permission to gently point out when our old thought seems to be hanging around again. In order for this to happen, of course, we have to make it a priority to surround ourselves with people who love us, who are good for our souls, and who have access to our authentic selves.

The sixth step is finding a song that expresses our new thought in music. Music not only embeds words in different areas of the brain.

The endorphins released when we sing (oxytocin and dopamine) enhance the neuroplasticity of the brain, boost our immune system, fight illness, depression, and strokes, and help us manage pain.

Finally, we must give our swapped-out thought time to fully make itself at home. Like any guest, it may take a few weeks to become part of our mental family. As it does, and we begin to feel the power of its truth, we must remember to express the thankfulness in our hearts for the transforming power of Christ's love.

Something to think about:

Take time to write down a thought you can't seem to shake. Follow the steps laid out in this devotional. How was that for you? Was there a place where you could have used some help?

Prayer

God of all Truth, I confess that I have believed _____, which I now realize is false and damaging. I renounce that thought and replace it with your thought, which is _____. I gently release myself from all the years I have unintentionally granted refuge to that thought. Thank you for the truth. Amen.

DAY TWENTY-EIGHT

Blessed is the man who walks not in the counsel of the wicked, nor stands in the way of sinners, nor sits in the seat of scoffers; but his delight is in the law of the LORD, and on his law he meditates day and night. He is like a tree planted by streams of water that yields its fruit in its season, and its leaf does not wither.

-- Ps. 1:1-3

Today's reading focuses on the positive effects of meditation. There are a variety of meditative practices with different benefits. For our purposes, I would define meditation as "thinking one thought to the exclusion of all others." This requires the development of inner discipline, training the mind to do what *you* want it to do.

Plato described the undisciplined state of our minds using the analogy of a ship in which the sailors made a mutiny and locked the captain and the navigator in the cabin below. One sailor after another—none of whom knows how to navigate—takes the wheel as the whim strikes him and steers for a while. The ship follows a completely random course. The task of a person, according to Plato, is to release the captain and the navigator and take control of the ship of our minds so that we can determine and steer toward our goals.

In our passage, the mutinous sailors are the random and unhelpful thoughts generated by the mental company we keep. I would summarize the "wicked," the "sinners," and the "scoffers" as any pattern of thinking that wants to keep us (a) agitated, (b) anxious, or (c) angry. Why? Because if someone can keep us agitated, anxious, or angry about something, we become easy to control. They can get us to buy things, see others in a negative light, or take some action that is to their advantage...not necessarily to ours.

The remedy is to meditate on the law of God. For Christians this law is summarized by Jesus as loving God with all our heart, soul, mind, and strength, and loving our neighbor as ourselves. Every other verse of the New Testament is intended to be an elaboration of this Greatest Commandment: love.

Meditating upon the law of love means thinking a thought from Scripture to the exclusion of all other thoughts. As a simple exercise, get yourself into a comfortable position in a space where you are not likely to be distracted. Set a timer for 10 minutes. Take a deep breath, and let it out slowly.

Then, take a phrase from today's reading and turn it into a personal affirmation: "I am like a tree planted by streams of water." Repeat this phrase over and over in your mind until the timer goes off. Other thoughts will try to take control of your thinking. This is normal. When it happens, gently bring your mind back to the phrase, "I am like a tree planted by streams of water." When the timer goes off, take another deep breath and let it out slowly.

Take a few moments to reflect on how that exercise made you feel. You may want to engage in this exercise every day for a week. At the end of that week, reflect again on how it affected you.

Our reading says that meditating on the law [love] of God "yields its fruit [benefits] in its season..." What are those fruits? Multiple studies reveal many benefits, but here are eight. Meditation...

1. Lowers stress.

2. Reduces anxiety.

3. Enhances mental health.

4. Improves self-awareness.

5. Increases concentration and attention span.

6. Reduces memory loss.

7. Generates empathy and kindness.

8. Improves sleep.

How long does it take for these benefits to kick in? The Bible doesn't sugarcoat the fact that it takes time: "It yields its fruit in its season." How long does it take a Palestinian fig tree to make a ripe fig? About two months. That's about how long it takes for meditation to begin to produce significant benefits in our lives.

You become what you read. You become what you listen to. You become what you watch. You become what you think. Choose wisely.

Something to think about:

How did the exercise explained above feel? What worked, and where were there any distractions? How do you think this could be helpful in your everyday spiritual practices?

Prayer

Loving God, I thank you for the love that is helping me take back my life from the inside out. Grant me wisdom in choosing my mental companions. Guide me as I select the thoughts from your Word on which to meditate. Give me both patience and perseverance to await the fruit of my spiritual practice that will come in its season. Finally, give me faith, the positive expectation that I will gradually recover to a life worth living. Amen.

DAY TWENTY-NINE

But this I call to mind, and therefore I have hope: The steadfast love of the LORD never ceases; his mercies never come to an end; they are new every morning...

-- Lam. 3:21-23

As we wake up each morning, we have many tasks that lie before us. However, our recovery process has only one goal. Stay spiritually sober: a calm spirit, a clear mind, and a loving heart. This means we must focus on today.

We will be defeated at the outset if we insist on dragging yesterday into today. Perhaps yesterday was a great day with much to celebrate. Perhaps we had a day or two when we did not think of suicide at all. We must not let that become an excuse for letting our guard down or abandoning our recovery work. It will be more helpful if we give thanks to God and others who have given us a measure of healing. We then turn our attention to what we need to do to make this a day of spiritual sobriety as well.

On the other hand, perhaps yesterday was a difficult day with many challenges. There may have been things we did not handle so well. We may have "fallen off the wagon." Instead of a calm spirit, we let anxiety get the upper hand. Instead of a clear mind, we admitted some negative thoughts or memories that led to confusion and rumination. Instead of a loving heart, we became self-absorbed, withdrawn, irritable, or short-tempered.

Dragging the residue from yesterday's missteps will not help you or anyone else. At best, it will sully the pure waters of this new day with anxiety, confusion, and egoism. At worst, it will make you want to quit. Remember, you can make many mistakes, but you are not a failure unless you quit.

In contrast to this yesterday-contaminating approach, God treats each day as a new beginning: "his mercies never come to an end; they are new every morning..." While we might be tempted to say to ourselves, "That's it. I've had it with you," God never does.

I remind myself of this every day when I am praying for healing in the lives of others that God has placed in my path. There is a moment of hesitation at the beginning as a vague sense of unworthiness casts its shadow across my soul. But then, the Holy Spirit reminds me: the mercies of God never come to an end and I can pray for others expectantly and in faith.

Unless we have someone to whom we should make amends, leave the mistakes of yesterday where they belong: yesterday. In the words of Ralph Waldo Emerson, "Finish each day and be done with it. You have done what you could. Some blunders and absurdities no doubt crept in; forget them as soon as you can."

For nearly twenty centuries, Christians have been reassuring themselves with the ancient words of St. Benedict: "Always we begin again." How well you have done your recovery work in the past does not matter. Have you been skipping these readings? It does not matter. Have you practiced a few days of meditation and quit? It does not matter. Have you indulged yourself in thoughts that are not good for your soul? It does not matter.

One thing matters. Begin again.

Something to think about:

What are some ways you can begin again? How do you leave things in the past where they belong? Are there friends or family that help along this path?

Prayer

Merciful God, we thank you for your everlasting patience with us, which makes each day new. I confess the temptation to allow the sludge of the past to sully the pure water of this new day. With your help, I choose to leave the successes and mistakes of my yesterdays in the past. Grant me the grace to live this day with renewed strength, fresh hope, and positive expectation that good things will come my way. Amen.

DAY THIRTY

Honor doctors for their services, since indeed the Lord created them...The Lord created medicines out of the earth, and a sensible person won't ignore them. With those medicines, the doctor cures and takes away pain. Those who prepare oint-ments will make a compound out of them, and their work will never be finished, and well-being spreads over the whole world from them. My child, when you are sick, don't look around elsewhere, but pray to the Lord, and he will heal you. And give doctors a place, because the Lord created them also, and don't let them leave you, because you indeed need them. There's a time when success is in their hands as well.

-- Sirach 38:1-15 (excerpted)

The book of Sirach was written by Ben Sira during the time between the Old and New Testaments, around 200 BC. It is included in the Bibles of Catholics, Eastern Orthodox, and Oriental Orthodox Christians, and was originally included in a separate section of the King James Bible.

While not giving it the status of other books in the Bible, many Protestants value its practical wisdom, but do not apply the teachings of the book to establish any doctrine. It is similar to other wisdom books of the Bible like the book of Proverbs. It is where the spiritual rubber meets the road of reality.

The Bible generally speaks positively about physicians. Luke, the writer of Acts and the Gospel, given his name, is referred to by Paul as "the beloved physician." His writing often uses medical terms that only a physician would know. Jesus refers to himself as a physician of the soul. When he could do no miracles in his hometown, he referred to himself as a physician who could not heal himself.

On the other hand, the Scripture is generally critical of a medical approach that ignores the spiritual aspect of healing. The Old Testament notes that when King Asa became ill, "... even in his disease he did not seek the LORD, but sought help [only] from physicians." Jesus heals a woman who had a flow of blood for twelve years, had spent all her living on physicians, and had suffered much but grew no better. She was not the first nor the last person to be bankrupted by a medical condition. Next to losing one's job, medical expenses are the number one reason for bankruptcy in the United States.

We may assume that when the New Testament emphasizes the importance of spiritual healing, it is with the implicit understanding that medical practitioners also have a role to play. Today's reading from the book of Sirach makes this integrated approach explicit: "My child, when you are sick, don't look around elsewhere, but pray to the Lord, and he will heal you. And give doctors a place…"

There is a place for a physician for some of us who are recovering from suicidal thinking. Forty-six percent of those who die by suicide have a diagnosed mental health issue, often inadequately treated.[5] We may be dealing with a brain disorder that can be effectively addressed with a pharmacological or electroconvulsive treatment. In the words of our reading, "Those who prepare ointments will make a compound out of them, and their work will never be finished, and well-being spreads over the whole world from them."

The reading admonishes us not to avoid these potential remedies by "looking around elsewhere." We must be self-aware of any pride or prejudice that would set us off on a wild goose chase of other lesser remedies simply out of stubbornness. Focusing only on spiritual remedies to the exclusion of medical ones can be just as ill-advised as ignoring the spiritual component of healing and expecting a medication to solve all our problems.

---

5   https://www.nami.org/about-mental-illness/com-mon-with-mental-illness/risk-of-suicide/

Ultimately, our healing lies in our surrender to the will of God, and a willingness to follow that will, wherever it might lead us.

Something to think about:

How would you use this integrated approach to your overall health? What are some of the things you are neglecting, physically or mentally? What is your action plan to move in a healthier direction?

Prayer

Healing God, as I discern the course of my recovery and the resources I will need, I pray for your guidance. Grant that I might know the proper role that medical professionals, physicians, nurses, pharmacists, and physician assistants play in my healing. Help me avoid the twin temptations of expecting a medical miracle to solve all my spiritual problems on the one hand or falling prey to a pride-driven refusal to get help on the other. I surrender to your will and I listen for your guidance however it might come. Amen.

DAY THIRTY-ONE

...so that we may no longer be children, tossed to and fro by the waves and carried about by every wind of doctrine, by human cunning, by craftiness in deceitful schemes. Rather, speaking the truth in love, we are to grow up...

-- Eph. 4:14-15

When the Spirit of truth comes, he will guide you into all the truth...

-- John 16:13

Every human being has a spot in their field of vision where they are totally blind. This "blind spot" is caused by a discontinuity in the retina, where the optic nerve enters the back of the eye. As a result, there are actually two black holes in our visual field, one created by our left eye and the second by our right eye.

What is perhaps even more interesting than the blind spot is how the human brain manages these holes in our visual field. It does not allow us to see them. The brain fills in our blind spots with information that is consistent with whatever else is in our visual field at the time. It continually Photoshops what we are looking at. It fools us into thinking we are seeing everything clearly. In reality, we are not, and we don't know that we are not. We don't know what we don't know.

We have similar blind spots in other parts of our lives. The blind spot on our driver's side, when another car is just to the left of our rear bumper, can get us into real trouble. The brain incorrectly fills in what it cannot see in the mirror. More than 800,000 blind spot accidents happen each year.

We all have similar blind spots in our perceptions of ourselves and our life situation which can also get us into real trouble. We live burdened with anxieties that are rooted in beliefs that are simply false. We make flawed decisions because those decisions are based on incomplete or inaccurate information. Life becomes like a bumper car where we can't see what is hitting us over and over again. Today's reading describes this as being tossed to and fro.

Our blind spot can make us naïve regarding other people; we become easily fooled. We keep wondering why these things are happening to us. It may convince us that suicide is the only way out by concealing other possible solutions in our blind spot. In order to recover, we need to shrink our blind spot. But how?

Jesus said that the truth will set us free. Here is the reality: God's truth will often come through another person. The person through whom God speaks may be a business associate, a trusted friend, or a life partner. It may be through a person going through a similar situation or an individual in a support group.

In 2021, my son, Michael, reconnected with me after years of estrangement. He had become addicted to opioids and was living in a shelter. Shortly after reconnecting, I joined an Alanon group. I walked into the first meeting filled with anxiety that Michael might die of an overdose. I would not be able to survive that.

The man who spoke in my first meeting described a situation in which his daughter was addicted and living on the streets in another state. Then he said something I will never forget.

"I have come to the place where I know that if I get a call that Margo has died, I will be able to accept it. It will break my heart, but I will be OK."

Those words shot through me like an electric current. They lifted the great burden of fear off my shoulders. I had thought I could not survive if anything were to happen to Michael. I was wrong. Now, I could put him into God's hands. With God's help, I could do anything.

A few months later, I received the call that every parent dreads. Michael had died of an overdose. And I was heartbroken. But I survived. I knew that God had spoken to me through a member of the group that very first night. What he shared had set me free.

Sometimes the truth we need will come from a skilled counselor, a therapist, spiritual director, or pastoral counselor. The truth we need may not always be easy to hear. When a truth has been hidden in our blind spot, it will often feel a little odd at first.

In any case, we want to keep an open mind. When someone you trust speaks a word that may be an unfamiliar truth, take some time to reflect on it. Ask the Holy Spirit to reveal the truth to you. Jesus said that this is the Holy Spirit's job, to guide us into truth.

Let us open our hearts and minds to the Spirit's truth and shrink that blind spot one day at a time.

Something to think about:

Often, we do not see our blind spots. Who in your life can help you work through seeing clearer when your blind spots get in the way? Why would you pick this person?

Prayer

Holy, helping, healing Spirit, I open my heart and mind to you. There are many conflicting voices in the world and sometimes in my own mind as well that toss me to and fro. You have promised to lead me into truth. Please reveal to me those wise, trustworthy voices who can speak the truth to me in love. When I am tempted to react defensively, remind me that your love for me is unfailing and that your words of truth are always spoken, not to put me down, but to help grow me up into all that I can be. Thank you. Amen.

DAY THIRTY-TWO

If I am to live in the flesh, that means fruit-ful labor for me. Yet which I shall choose I cannot tell. I am hard-pressed between the two. My desire is to depart and be with Christ, for that is far better. But to remain in the flesh is more necessary on your account. Convinced of this, I know that I will remain and continue with you all, for your progress and joy in the faith, so that in me you may have ample cause to glory in Christ Jesus, because of my coming to you again.

-- Phil. 1:22-26

Sin demands to have a man [or woman] by himself. It withdraws him from the community. The more isolated a person is, the more destructive will be the power of sin over him, and the more deeply he becomes involved in it, the more disastrous his isolation. -- *Dietrich Bonhoeffer*

At the point when he wrote today's reading, Paul is likely sixty years of age, elderly for a person of his time. In the thirty years since his conversion, Paul has experienced some difficult days. He has endured countless beatings, been shipwrecked three times, and stoned nearly to death. He often has had to go without food or water. He has shivered through sleepless nights without adequate clothing to keep warm.

His suffering is not all behind him. As he writes these verses, he sits in a Roman prison, unsure of what additional challenges any day might bring. While the book of Philippians is the most joyful of any of his writings, we sense a certain weariness in the old soul. He begins to reflect on his death.

We hear in his words what many of us have felt, especially as we age: an ambivalence toward living. A part of him wants to live, and a part of him wants to die.

All that he has experienced in life has begun to weigh on him. I find this particularly true among older adults. As the years mount, so do the losses, and every day seems to bring word of new ones. The elderly Apostle writes honestly about this: "My desire is to depart and be with Christ..." When he adds, "for that is far better," he may have in mind the many souls he has loved and missed who now await a reunion on the other side.

And, yet, there is another part of Paul that wants to live, and the part of him that wants to live is focused on a purpose yet to be served: "If I am to live in the flesh, that means fruitful labor for me." Here, he's not talking about a job that pays money. He is referring to those who need him and for whom he has great affection: "But to remain in the flesh is more necessary on your account."

Paul is bringing to light the inner conversation that many of us have as we age. Unfortunately, most of us do not have either the self-confidence or a community where we feel safe enough to speak these thoughts. More tragically, the isolation of many leads to their actual deaths. The highest suicide rates by far are among folks Paul's age and, for white men, even older.

Paul remembers what is easy for us to forget, especially as we age: our lives matter. He resolves his dilemma on the side of living: "I know that I will remain and continue with you all, for your progress and joy in the faith, so that in me you may have ample cause to glory in Christ Jesus, because of my coming to you again."

Our lives matter, more than we know. To matter is a two-edged sword. If we are going to bask in the warmth of human affection that gives such meaning to our lives, then we must also be willing to accept the responsibility of doing damage should we leave them in a violent exit.

Certainly, it is always possible for any of us, by either act of will or sheer neglect, to unravel our lives to a point where we may convince ourselves and perhaps a few others that we do not matter, but that is disfigurement of the very essence of human connection.

I find that when we are able to speak our thoughts aloud to someone who really listens, most of us are able to do what Paul did: talk ourselves into living.

For those of us on the road to recovery from suicidal thinking, the challenge of today's reading is two-fold. First, let us find a community, even of two or three, with whom we can share these thoughts. Second, let us summon our courage to speak them. In doing so, we may not only recommit to our lives but also, unwittingly, save another.

Something to think about:

What can help you summon your inner strength to start these conversations? Is God present in this conversation?

Prayer

Eternal God, I thank you for the home you have prepared for me in the life to come, and the promise of rest in a state of being where you will wipe all tears from every eye, and death shall be no more, nor mourning, nor crying, nor sorrow shall be any more. But I remain in this world, for there are those ones I am called to love, lessons to learn, and experiences to share. Help me accept my ponderings about living and dying as signs of a vital spiritual engagement, and to liberate others as I speak with courage. Amen.

DAY THIRTY-THREE

Is anyone among you sick? Let him call for the elders of the church, and let them pray over him, anointing him with oil in the name of the Lord. And the prayer of faith will save the one who is sick, and the Lord will raise him up.

-- James 5:14-15

There is simply too much research to cite indicating that a spiritual perspective and practice has a positive impact on both our physical and mental health. Spirituality has been demonstrated to play an important role in treating both medical and psychological conditions. Any form of psychotherapy exploring the depth of the human psyche will eventually reach the spiritual domain.

Thirty-one significant research studies provide empirical evidence of the benefits of spirituality to individuals experiencing various psychological conditions such as anxiety, eating disorders, depression, and stress. In many cases, a spiritual perspective and practice have been shown to be as effective as some medications—without the side effects.

More specifically, involvement in a faith community can be protective against suicidal thinking and behavior. For those of us recovering from suicidal thinking, it is important to know that participation in the religious practices of a faith community is associated with lower levels of both suicidal ideation and a history of suicide attempts.

These studies indicate that medical science is beginning to catch up with the ancient wisdom of traditions thousands of years old including the one we read today. The standard practice in the early church, when someone was ill or injured, was to seek out those of spiritual maturity and ask for anointing and prayer. This was understood as simply an extension of the healing ministry of Jesus, which is now present in believers through the working of the Holy Spirit.

As mentioned earlier, these kinds of spiritual practices can be as effective as some medications. A question might be framed like this: "I am holding a pill in my hand that has been shown to be effective in improving the health of body and mind. It costs nothing, has no side effects, and you can't overdose. In addition, you can add it to any medications you are now taking [don't stop taking them!] without harmful interactions. Would you take it?"

That "pill" is healing prayer.

I have gone through seasons in my life when I would find and attend a weekly healing service with prayers and anointing with oil, usually. I would go forward to ask for prayer every time it was offered. I looked at it as a dose of healing. Over six months, I probably received over twenty doses of spiritual healing.

If you are recovering from suicidal thinking, I would encourage you to consider making anointing with oil and prayer one component of your healing process. What are the benefits?

- It gets you out of your home, which has been shown to be good for your mental health—especially if you get a little exercise.

- It eases you into an interaction with other people without requiring a lot of conversation on your part—unless you want it.

- It provides an opportunity for a therapeutic touch from another human being (placing oil on your forehead), which also has been shown to be good for us—unless we are dealing with PTSD from a past incidence of abuse.

- As already mentioned, the therapeutic value of healing prayer is significant in and of itself.

One of the obstacles that can stand in the way of any involvement in a faith community is differences in belief. Here is what is interesting. Involvement in a faith community can be protective against both suicidal thinking and behavior regardless of the belief system. Try to put your critical thinking aside temporarily and breathe in the healing potential of the spiritual experience of being with others who are doing the best that they can.

Finally, be wise in how you ask for prayer. Unless someone is trained to deal with suicide, they may not know how to deal with a request for healing from suicidal thoughts. Simply indicate you are in a recovery process and ask for another dose of healing.

If your intuition leads you to share more, trust it. You are probably strong enough to handle whatever happens next, and what happens next may turn out to be an unexpected blessing.

Something to think about:

What obstacles are getting in your way? Do you have spiritual practices that involve people and can be a place of healing?

Prayer

Healing Lord, I thank you that when my mind feels weak and my heart feels broken, my legs still work, my feet can still walk, and my voice can still form the words, "Pray for me." As I take these steps in the direction of healing prayer, guide each one of them in the direction they should go. Look upon my willingness as a sign of my faith, a faith made great not by the straining of my will but by following my heart, from the desert of despair into the hope for better days ahead. Amen.

DAY THIRTY-FOUR

And on the Sabbath he began to teach in the synagogue, and many who heard him were astonished, saying, "Where did this man get these things?...Is not this the carpenter, the son of Mary and brother of James and Joses and Judas and Simon? And are not his sisters here with us?" And he could do no mighty work there...

-- Mark 6:2-3,5

Jesus was no magician. In ancient terms, a magician was one who had the power to invoke supernatural forces with effects in the natural world. Magicians did not require a believing community for their magic to work. Their powers lay solely within themselves. The classic image of a magician is the solitary figure alone in a dark room, conjuring spells or mixing potions in a cauldron.

However, we might understand Jesus as the Son of God; his power was fully released only in the presence of a believing community. An atmosphere of skepticism, suspicion, or frivolity is spiritual kryptonite for anyone, even for Jesus. In the face of these toxins, "he could do no mighty work there." One verse later, he is gone.

In praying for our recovery, it is important to find a spiritual community that cultivates an atmosphere of positive expectation regarding healing, even a community of two or three. What are the elements of positive expectation?

- The community gives concrete expression to the belief that the healing ministry of Jesus continues among them through the power of his Spirit. This includes regular opportunities in its public ministry to offer healing prayer for individuals.

- The faith of the community in the working of God is fortified through the preaching, teaching, and testimony of the church.

- The community's understanding of healing encompasses the whole person in all the dimensions of life: physical, emotional, and spiritual.

- Healing ministry is understood to be an integrated partnership among spiritual practitioners, lifestyle advisors, and medical professionals.

- The cultivation of a positive expectation of Divine healing, in whatever form, is understood to be a joint responsibility of both the community and the individual. Sometimes, our spiritual reserves are so low that we must borrow the faith of others.

Ironically, one of the greatest obstacles to an atmosphere of positive expectation is familiarity. The fact that Jesus's neighbors know all about him, his history, his occupation, and his family makes it impossible for the people of his hometown to expect anything extraordinary. In fact, their focus on the ordinariness of his life becomes an obstacle to anything extraordinary happening.

One of the strongest testimonies to the normalcy of Jesus's childhood is the fact that his hometown could not see anything unusual about him *at all*. If, as some books suggest, the child Jesus demonstrated supernatural powers like creating living birds out of clay or killing other children with a curse, then his community would not have been surprised by his claims as an adult to possess unusual powers.

God still uses ordinary people, flaws and all, to channel healing into our lives. We must cultivate a sincere expectancy that prayers for our healing will result in some positive effect. Those positive effects can result in physical changes, but they can also include relief from emotional distress, deeper insight into the source(s) of our pain, further guidance for our healing process, or reaffirmation of God's loving presence with us. If we are open and expectant, something almost always happens in the hours and days following a prayer for healing if we are ready to receive it.

We do not receive what we simply want. We receive what we pray for, expect, recognize when it arrives, and give thanks for. This is the true magic of our faith: when we connect with God and one another in a community of expectation, extraordinary things begin to happen.

Something to think about:

Write a prayer that includes how change comes from within, positivity, with the help of the community.

Prayer

Lord, guide me into a community of positive expectation for my healing, even a community of two or three. Create in me that same positive faith, that together, we might pray for healing with expectation, and look for the relief, the insight, the guidance, or the reassurance that will come as an answer. When that answer comes, open my eyes to recognize it, my heart to give thanks for it, and my mind to remember it. Amen.

"When I pray, coincidences happen. When I don't, they don't." -- *Archbishop William Temple*

DAY THIRTY-FIVE

Then they said to him, "What shall we do to you, that the sea may quiet down for us?" For the sea grew more and more tempestuous. He said to them, "Pick me up and hurl me into the sea; then the sea will quiet down for you, for I know it is because of me that this great tempest has come upon you." And the Lord appointed a great fish to swallow up Jonah. And Jonah was in the belly of the fish three days and three nights.

-- Jonah 1:11-12, 17

The book of Jonah is one of my favorite books of the Bible. In its four short chapters, it tells the story of a man who resists and runs from his life's purpose, gets himself into trouble on a sailing ship, and is saved from drowning by a large fish where he relents and accepts his purpose, but at the end is left with a choice: will he accept the incredibly merciful nature of God, or will he insist that people "get what is coming to them," which leaves him miserable and wanting to die.

Now is probably a good time to talk about the power of symbol in the Bible. I believe the story of Jonah is spiritually symbolic. Many people think that makes the story less significant. Actually, the opposite is the case. If the story is literal history, we are reading the account of a single individual who lived millennia ago, much like we would read the story of a Neanderthal man whose remains have been recently excavated from a cave in Portugal. We smile, close our browsers, and go on with our day.

If, however, the book of Jonah is spiritually symbolic, it tells a story about all of us. We each have a purpose to which we tend to be resistant or indifferent; we get into trouble by one means or another, and God sends a means of rescue, which gives us an opportunity to embrace our life rather than run from it. How we end up at the end depends largely on whether we can come to grips with a merciful God...or insist on a punitive one. This is how I understand Jonah. I take him seriously, but not literally.

God calls Jonah to go preach in Nineveh, a city in trouble, like many cities today. But Jonah boards a boat to Tarshish, 180 degrees in the opposite direction. When a storm arises on the sea, and it becomes apparent that Jonah is the reason, Jonah's suicidal thinking begins to emerge. Rather than embracing his life's purpose, he chooses to drown. Unable to make the decision himself, he asks the sailors to throw him into the sea, a form of "suicide by sailor."

His suicide attempt fails. He is swallowed by a large fish that saves his life. The fish is God's love reaching out to him. It is the miracle that gives him a second chance.

By some mystery of destiny, the stories of many of us are like Jonah's. We have our own "fish story" which is not so much about the big one that got away, but the one that came along at just the right moment and saved us.

I have heard so many of these that I would not know which one to tell. A person downs a bottle of pills and waits to die only to have a friend drop by for a visit, unexpected and seemingly random. In an act of desperation, a man drives his car head-long into a tree. He should not survive, but he does. A woman removes her husband's gun from the gun cabinet to take her life. But while she is loading it, the phone rings. When she answers it, she hears the voice of her pastor checking in on her, an intuition on his part. She hangs up and gives her life to God instead.

Among those who take this literally, there is always a search for a fish large enough to swallow a person whole. For me, as one who takes this seriously, there is always a search in someone's history for that random coincidental moment, God's great fish, that is large enough to hold their story with all its sorrow...and save them.

We are sent into the world with an unfolding purpose: work to do, someone to love, lessons to learn, experiences to share. We can resist that purpose, run from that purpose, or deny that purpose. For some of us, the consequences of that resistance will lead us into suicidal thinking. That thinking is not God's way of punishing us. It is our way of punishing ourselves. It is the sea into which we toss ourselves.

Today, I would ask you to remember that great fish in your story and give it its due. There is someone or something that has happened to you, amidst all the sorrow and pain, that carries this great, life-saving love. We always have the choice in our recovery. We can focus on the difficult tasks we have had to endure, the stormy, sea-sickening swells crashing against us over and over again, and our fellow sailors who are suffering from some of our choices.

Or we can focus on the Great Fish of God's love that came to us at just the right time. And who knows, perhaps today's reading is just the Great Fish you need to get through another day.

Something to think about:

What is your GREAT FISH? How do we hear God's calling, and what happens when we ignore it?

Prayer

God of creatures great and small, amidst all the losses, pain, and sorrow I have known, some by my own doing, some by running from my real life, help me focus on the Great Fish of your love and the ways it has appeared. Only this love is large enough to swallow my pain and confusion and, yes, even my rebellion against my life's purpose. Today, bring this love to mind, and when it appears out of the depths of my remembrances, help me to rest in it once again. Amen.

DAY THIRTY-SIX

Jonah, however, was greatly displeased, and he became angry. So he prayed to the Lord, saying, "O Lord, is this not what I said while I was still in my own country? This is why I was so quick to flee toward Tarshish. I knew that you are a gracious and compassionate God, slow to anger, abounding in loving devotion—one who relents from sending disaster. And now, O Lord, please take my life from me, for it is better for me to die than to live."

-- Jonah 4:1-3

We come to the last chapter of the book of Jonah. In the first chapter, Jonah asks to be drowned, a suicide-by-sailor. In today's reading, months later, Jonah wants to die yet again. As a person recovering from suicidal thinking, I find this reading extremely realistic and, therefore, encouraging.

For many of us, suicidal thinking is not like a head cold that we get over in a week or two. While it may be triggered by an unbearable circumstance or a series of them, it often establishes a pattern in our thinking as a coping mechanism. During times of relative calm, it goes dormant. But when life becomes too painful or overwhelming, suicide reemerges as an option. In our minds, we say to ourselves, "I can always kill myself."

In our story, Jonah has successfully accomplished his mission. He has completed a preaching mission in a city so large that it required a three-day journey just to cross it. The citizens responded: "And the Ninevites believed God. They proclaimed a fast and dressed in sackcloth, from the greatest of them to the least. When word reached the king of Nineveh, he got up from his throne, took off his royal robe, covered himself with sackcloth, and sat in ashes."

Yet, Jonah is not happy in his success. Nineveh was the capital of the Assyrian Empire, Israel's most hated enemy. His proclamation that God would destroy the city in forty days would bring him no small satisfaction. It would be equivalent to preaching hellfire and damnation to people you really don't like anyway. Some might call it love, but inside, they may actually be quite pleased with God's judgment of another.

The fact that God relented from destroying the Ninevites sent Jonah into a rage, and it was this rage turned inward that fueled his desire to die. Throughout the course of the book, Jonah has not been able to address a fundamental issue in his life. Focusing on dying becomes his "go-to" when his rage gets the better of him, and his rage gets the better of him when life doesn't work the way he thinks it should.

My good friend, Michelle Snyder, shares this insight: "People often say they are confused. Actually, they are rarely confused. They are crystal clear. They just don't like what they see."

Jonah doesn't like what he sees. Life doesn't work the way he wants it to. Do we not relate to that? Employers fire us. People reject us. Health fails us. Cruel people sometimes seem to get away with it.

How does Jonah cope with it all? He starts wanting to die. That is his pattern. It is his go-to means of coping with his rage. At the end of the book, he is in the same place he was at the beginning. He has no real future because his future is just a repeat of his past.

There is another option besides death for Jonah. He can stop trying to run the world and surrender to the God who created it. Jonah can change this thinking pattern, and so can we. When life disappoints us, and we find the flame of an inner rage beginning to grow, we can surrender to God's will instead of our rage.

Something to think about:

How do you stop trying to run the world and surrender to God? What are the things getting in the way? How can you turn your sails to catch the Holy Spirit?

Prayer

Dear God, life often does not work the way I want it to, and parts of my life have not turned out as I planned. In this moment of honesty, I confess that I find myself angry, even brought to the point of rage. My way of dealing with my rage has been to think of suicide. I now realize that this is simply my resistance to your will for my life. I am powerless and my life is unmanageable without your love and guidance. Instead of fantasizing about death, I surrender to your will for my life. Heal this rage inside me. Such as I am, take me and use me in your service. Guide and direct my ways and show me what to do for you. Amen.

DAY THIRTY-SEVEN

As the sun was rising, God appointed a scorching east wind, and the sun beat down on Jonah's head so that he grew faint and wished to die, saying, "It is better for me to die than to live." Then God asked Jonah, "Have you any right to be angry about the plant?" "I do," he replied. "I am angry enough to die!" But the Lord said, "You cared about the plant, which you neither tended nor made grow. It sprang up in a night and perished in a night. So should I not care about the great city of Nineveh, which has more than 120,000 people who cannot tell their right hand from their left, and many cattle as well?"

-- Jonah 4:1-3

Jonah is only one of two books of the Bible that ends in a question: should God care about a city of 120,000 people who are not of the right faith and have not lived with the right behaviors? In the words of the New Testament should God so love the world, the entire world?

This question is posed to Jonah.

From one perspective, Jonah's life has been a series of unlucky breaks. The book begins with God telling him to "get up," which may have been an indication he was bedridden by a sullen mood. He boards a ship that nearly sinks in a storm, placing the entire crew in mortal peril. He takes a public position that a city is going to be destroyed in forty days—and it isn't. He finds shade under a plant from the searing heat of the sun, and a worm destroys it, leaving him without protection.

From one standpoint, Jonah is an ill-begotten soul who not only has bad luck but who also brings bad luck to those around him. In fact, to be designated "a Jonah" by a ship's crew came to mean a person on shipboard regarded as the cause of ill luck, a person whose presence is supposed or alleged to cause misfortune. Later, in games of chance, "a Jonah" was the name attached to a player who could never win anything. That's certainly one way to look at Jonah's life story. One bad stroke of luck after another that leaves him wanting to die.

But there is another way of telling his story. Everything that has happened in his life to this point has *not* been designed to make him want to die. In fact, God doesn't criticize Jonah for wanting to die. God gets right to the root of it all by asking this final question.

Is it right for God to care about everyone? Is it right for God to love the world? That's the question for Jonah. It is not a stretch to believe that one of the reasons that Jonah was born into the world in the first place was to answer this question.

As a person who has been interested in spiritual healing for decades, I have read about and seen with my own eyes people from every background experience the love of God through a healing touch of one kind or another. Some have been conservative Christians, some quite progressive; some have been Christians who don't believe in spiritual healing at all—until it happened to them. Some have been of the Islamic faith, some Judaism, some Buddhist. Some have been atheists who have reluctantly agreed to allow someone to pray for them. I have been forced to a conclusion: God loves us all, and loves us all profoundly.

We can each look at our lives through a "Jonah" lens: bad luck, one bad thing after another happening to us. Or we may realize that it has all been used to bring us to a significant question: "Can we accept that God loves us all, and loves us all profoundly?"

If Jonah can embrace a "yes" to that question, a transformative chain reaction will be set in motion. He can accept the Ninevites as beloved. If he can love the Ninevites, he can love the Ninevite inside himself (there is always one there). If he can accept the Ninevites as beloved, he can stop raging against them. If he can stop raging, he can stop wanting to die. His life begins to make sense, not because it was easy, but because it was bringing him to this point of spiritual revelation.

He now knows why he needed to run from God by taking a boat to Tarshish, why he needed to be thrown off a boat on the verge of being shipwrecked, why he needed to spend three days and nights in the gullet of a fish, why he needed to be publicly humiliated by his message of destruction which turned out to be false. It was all necessary for him to answer at the level of his marrow the question: "Can I accept that God loves us all, and loves us all profoundly?"

The author of this powerful story does not record Jonah's answer. It is not really Jonah's answer he cares about. It is ours. It is our answer that will set our course, our answer that will set off a transformative chain of rethinking our lives. And, for those of us recovering from suicidal thinking, it is part of what will arrest our chain of suicidal thinking.

Can I accept that God loves us all, loves us profoundly, and loves me unreservedly?

God waits for that answer.

Something to think about:

How would you answer the questions God is asking? Is it right for God to care about everyone? Is it right for God to love the world?

Prayer

Loving God, I sometimes find it easiest to think of my life through the "Jonah" lens, a series of meaningless circumstances that have struck me one after another. But perhaps my life has been one effort after another to bring me to this point, where I accept the deep love you have, not only for the world you have made but for me personally. I now open myself to that love and pray that you will allow it to permeate the deepest regions of my soul. Let that love set off a chain reaction in my heart, where resistance becomes acceptance, where judgment becomes love, where raging becomes serenity, and where wanting to die gives way to a purpose for living. Thank you for loving me. Amen.

DAY THIRTY-EIGHT

Then when Judas, his betrayer, saw that Jesus was condemned, he changed his mind and brought back the thirty pieces of silver to the chief priests and the elders, saying, "I have sinned by betraying innocent blood." They said, "What is that to us? See to it yourself." And throwing down the pieces of silver into the temple, he departed, and he went and hanged himself.

-- Matt. 27:3-5

The tragic story of Judas illuminates one of the major issues we must deal with in recovering from suicidal thinking: shame.

Shame and guilt are different. Guilt is a failure of God's standard, a failure to love in one form or another. Shame is a failure of a community, family, or personal standard. We can feel shame without actually being guilty. An adolescent who can't afford name-brand clothing may feel shame before her peers, but she is not guilty. And we can be guilty without feeling shame. A person who cuts off another driver out of spite may be guilty but feel no shame at all.

Dealing with guilt before God is relatively clean. A process of self-examination, being honest about our failures, receiving forgiveness, offering restitution where indicated, and making amends as appropriate, these are the ways we deal with guilt. As we have already seen in the story of Jonah, God's loving devotion extended to an entire city of persons who undoubtedly had failed in ways large and small. Yet they were forgiven.

But shame, the painful feeling of humiliation or distress caused by failing the standards of ourselves or others can abide long after God has forgiven us and removed our guilt. Shame can be a poison to our souls. In order to recover, we must face the issue of shame head on.

As we see in the story of Judas, shame is intensified depending upon the manner of our perceived failure. Below is a list of the factors that intensify our shame:

   a. The degree to which our perceived failure is threatening our closest relationships and social network. Judas's actions would have had a profound, negative impact on his relationship to folks with whom he had spent more than two years sharing daily life. Shame can lead to estrangement and isolation, heightening our suicidal risk.

b. The irreversibility of our actions. Since Judas's tipping off the authorities to Jesus's meeting location led to his death, the consequences were irreversible. When we steal something we can return it. When we say something hurtful, we can make amends. But when someone dies, a career is ruined, or our children suffer from mistakes of our parenting that we cannot erase, the shame is intensified.

c. The degree to which our failure is public in nature. Judas's action would have become known to a wide range of people, beginning with the disciples but also extending to the military, religious leaders he was communicating with, and members of the general population. When our failures become publicly known through the media, legal system, or informal grapevines, it results in a loss of community esteem, which intensifies our shame.

d. An unrealistic need to please others. We don't know if this was an issue for Judas, but we know that Jesus warned us with the words, "Woe to you when all persons speak well of you." An excessive need to please others can be rooted in the way we were parented, genetics, the influences and pressures of society, or our choices along the way. When we feel we must please everyone, any displeasure from others results in feelings of shame.

e. Living in a system which self-regulates using shame. A family, organization, or business that uses the fear of disapproval to keep people in line intensifies feelings of shame among its members. A mafia culture is not guilt-based. It is shame-based. Many faith communities can be as well.

Shame is one of the most powerful motivations for suicidal thinking. Unlike guilt, which has a clear remedy, shame does not. It easily becomes that unbearable experience that suicide promises to help us escape.

It is important to note that Judas actually took all the steps the law required. We read that he repented ("changed his mind"), confessed his wrongdoing ("I have sinned by betraying innocent blood"), and made restitution ("brought back the thirty pieces of silver"). He is notably absent from the trial proceedings, so he obviously refused to turn state's evidence and testify against Jesus as well.

Here lies a critical point in our recovery process. It is shame that threatens to kill us, not guilt. Long after our guilt has been forgiven by God, our shame can continue to fuel our humiliation, self-degradation, and self-destructive thinking.

This is aggravated by the way we are treated by others, especially those who have used us for their own interests or who deny our humanity. Judas gets no help from the very religious leaders who were spiritually responsible for helping him deal with his guilt and shame. Their response was callous and cruel: "What is that to us? See to it yourself." It ramped up his shame at his most vulnerable moment.

Suicide was not inevitable for Judas. Peter, who denied even knowing Jesus failed in a similar way. He weeps bitterly, we are told, but he doesn't confess his failure or take any other step toward making amends. Yet, Jesus forgave Peter, reconciled their relationship, and reinstated him in a leadership position.

What was the main difference between Judas and Peter? Judas gave up too soon. If he had only stayed around a few more days, he would have given Jesus time to help overcome his shame.

Whatever our failure, God has embraced us with love and grace. We must give God time to snatch us from the jaws of shame.

Something to think about:

How has shame affected your life? Is it a key instigator in how you think of yourself? When do you find it happening the most? What is something you can do to counter these feelings by pushing them aside?

Prayer

Merciful God, stand with me in this moment and reassure me of your love as I explore the sources of any shame in my life. Give me clarity of heart and mind that I might discern the line between guilt and shame. For what do I feel shame? What intensifies my shame? How does shame feel like an unbearable circumstance in my life that I cannot escape? I now set my intention to refuse the destructive voices of shame, to shed them like the poisonous vipers they are, and to give you time to deliver me from their power. Amen.

DAY THIRTY-NINE

...let us run with endurance the race that is set before us, looking to Jesus, the founder and perfecter of our faith, who for the joy that was set before him endured the cross, despising the shame, and is seated at the right hand of the throne of God.

-- Heb. 12:1-2

Jesus despised shame. It is difficult to find stronger language throughout the entire New Testament. He despised the humiliation of hanging naked on a cross, being mocked and ridiculed, beaten and spat upon. He despised it.

There is every indication that Jesus also despised the effects of shame on the people he spent most of his time with: those who allegedly drank too much, ate too much, made their living as sex workers or by defrauding others, people whose failures were big and public.

He was accused of being a friend of sinners, but it might be more accurate to say that he was a friend of the shamed. He had watched the impact that shame had on their lives, even after they had changed their ways and been forgiven. He saw how they were treated, whispered about, marginalized, dehumanized, and all the impacts of shame.

Jesus despised shame.

At its best, shame in small doses may contribute to pro-social behavior. At its worst, shame humiliates us for no good purpose. Long after we have taken every reasonable step to deal with our failures, it continues to punish us. It strips us naked while others appear faultless beneath their proper attire. It degrades our self-esteem. It monopolizes our thinking with ruminations over past events. It erodes trust. It poisons new relationships. It blocks creativity.

Jesus despised shame.

We watch shame turn people into emotional and spiritual beggars. People who make one mistake and are arrested now find themselves with a criminal record to which they will forever have to bow. Estranged parents who, in spite of their best intentions, made mistakes in their parenting find themselves repeatedly begging for a relationship with their adult children and grandchildren. People who fall in love with the wrong person can be branded with labels that follow them for the rest of their lives.

Jesus despised shame.

The Apostle Paul encourages us not to "be conformed to this world, but to be transformed by the renewal of your minds." One of the transformations required in our recovery process is that we resist shame's insistence that we despise ourselves and join Jesus in despising shame instead.

That begins with despising our shame instead of despising ourselves. Once we have taken every reasonable step to deal with our guilt before God, a guilt that every human carries in its own individual expression, then we must begin to forcibly address our own personal shame with intention and whole-heartedness.

Let us bolster our courage and consider these questions.

Before whom are we feeling shame? How is this shame impeding our ability to achieve significant goals? How is this shame affecting our mental, emotional, spiritual, and physical health? What role does this shame play in our suicidal thinking?

Jesus died *for* our sins, but he died *with* our shame. He shared that experience with us. Jesus calls us to *accept* him, and receive his forgiveness for our failures (sins). But he calls us to *join* him in despising shame. It is time for us to despise, loathe, abhor, detest, our shame.

We are not only called to despise the shame laid upon us; we are called to despise the shame laid upon others. Society continues to be a place where shame is assigned to those who have failed in certain ways. I call them the *damaged good* of society. They are in the image of God; at their core is a spark of goodness and Godfulness. However, their particular failures have resulted in their being treated as if they are a damaged package, unfit for delivery, or rejected at the door. Even after they have taken every reasonable step to deal with their guilt, make amends, and receive forgiveness, shame threatens to keep them isolated and judged. We are called to despise that shame as well.

Dealing with shame can be an essential part of our recovery process. Finding a community of other shame-despisers can strengthen our resolve, even if it is only two or three persons.

One of my seminary professors, Lewis Smedes, wrote, "We feel guilty for what we do. We feel shame for who we are."

We are beloved sons and daughters of God. Any voice, inner or outer, that argues otherwise must be opposed with every thread of our being.

Something to think about:

Before whom are we feeling shame? How is this shame impeding our ability to achieve significant goals? How is this shame affecting our mental, emotional, spiritual, and physical health? What role does this shame play in our suicidal thinking?

Prayer

Brother Jesus, thank you for despising the shame heaped upon your life and for despising the shame laid upon others. Give me humility, my Brother, to admit my failures, to make amends, and to change my ways. But, then, give me resolve to despise the humiliation of shame, to starve it of attention, to deplete it of thought, to stunt it by neglect, to poison it at its root. Finally, make me alert to others who bear these shackles of shame, that by my love and welcome back into the human family, those chains might at least be loosened. And may the light of your love shining at the core of our beings, better illumine the darkness of the world. Amen.

DAY FORTY

He [Jesus] also told this parable to some who trusted in themselves that they were righteous, and treated others with contempt: "Two men went up into the temple to pray, one a Pharisee and the other a tax collector. The Pharisee, standing by himself, prayed thus: 'God, I thank you that I am not like other men, extortioners, unjust, adulterers, or even like this tax collector. I fast twice a week; I give tithes of all that I get.' But the tax collector, standing far off, would not even lift up his eyes to heaven, but beat his breast, saying, 'God, be merciful to me, a sinner!' I tell you, this man went down to his house justified, rather than the other.

-- Luke 18:9-14

During a period of my life when I was devoting a significant amount of my time to learning about suicide prevention, I received a call from Dr. David Litts, who was heading up the national suicide prevention efforts in the Surgeon General's office.

"You know," he began, "we're learning more about suicide, and here is my takeaway. People commit suicide for many reasons, but it basically comes down to two. A loss of hope. A loss of social connection."

He went on to say, "And if the church of Jesus Christ can't do something about it, it should close its doors."

Few things damage hope and erode social connection as fast as the belief that one is alone in one's failures. Having spoken now before hundreds of people thousands of times, it is easy to look out upon their faces and believe that you alone are dealing with your particular flavor of sin.

But, as Jesus recognized, the opposite can often be the case in faith communities. Given our noble efforts to live upright and godly lives, it is easy for some to fool themselves into believing they are superior to others. And so, Jesus told his parable "to some who trusted in themselves that they were righteous, and treated others with contempt."

Notice in his parable that he lists specifically two areas of failure that are regarded as most shameful and shamed in his time and in ours as well: money (extortion/tax collector) and sexual impropriety (adultery). Faith communities are relatively tolerant of sins such as pride, hypocrisy, gluttony, divisiveness, gossip, self-righteousness, and the like. But misconduct related to sex or money quickly divides people into two groups, one superior to the other, one deserving of shame, and one deserving of self-congratulation.

For those of us recovering from suicidal thinking in which shame is the unbearable experience we are trying to escape, this can lead us to believe that we are defective in ways that few others are. But here is the truth: in any group of 100 typical American adults, it is estimated that:

- Three are in a physically abusive, intimate relationship
- Six are considering suicide
- Ten say they have no close friends
- 18 suffer from an anxiety disorder
- 20 have been divorced
- 20 regularly or often feel lonely
- 21 of the married women have had an affair, 8 of whose husbands never found out
- 26 say they have had a midlife crisis
- 27 have cut off the relationship with a family member
- 30 were arrested and have a criminal record
- 34 have zero savings and are one paycheck away from a disaster
- 36 of the married men have had an affair, 24 of whose wives never found out
- 90 have a major regret they live with

If everyone in a typical congregation were to wear a sign listing their experiences using the categories above, all the shame within its walls would evaporate almost instantly.

This, I believe, was one of the purposes of Jesus's parable. His criticism of the Pharisee was not intended to belittle him. That would simply be a reverse form of superiority. No, I believe it was intended to liberate him. When we feel we must continually justify ourselves by maintaining some sort of superior moral position over others, we bind ourselves to a chain every bit as heavy as that dragged about by Marley's ghost. When we do not feel loved, warts and all, it alienates us from others, from ourselves, and from God.

At the end of the day, it is probably not the self-aware, deeply-forgiven, profoundly-loved tax collector who might be wishing to be dead. It may be the Pharisee who believes he is only one step away from total rejection.

None of this gives us a reason to *excuse* ourselves, but it does give us a reason to *forgive* ourselves. And it gives us a reason to shake off the shame that is threatening our lives.

Something to think about:

Do you find yourself justifying yourself to others? Do you find yourself more like the Pharisee or tax collector, and why? How does God's grace play a role in all this?

Prayer

Gracious God, we thank you for your love, which embraces the entirety of our beings. Grant us enough security in that love to quickly confess our failures, large and small, and to know that we are forgiven. Also grant this, a knowing that we are never alone in our failures. In spite of the various facades that we all must wear by convention, help us realize that nothing has befallen us that is not common to others, and to know that we are part of a community of those who fall and rise again, sometimes in total secrecy. Amen.

DAY FORTY-ONE

But when Simon Peter saw it, he fell down at Jesus' knees, saying, "Depart from me, for I am a sinful man, O Lord." For he and all who were with him were astonished at the catch of fish that they had taken, and so also were James and John, sons of Zebedee, who were partners with Simon. And Jesus said to Simon, "Do not be afraid; from now on you will be catching men." And when they had brought their boats to land, they left everything and followed him.

-- Luke 5:8-11

From the verses immediately preceding today's reading, we can reasonably assume that Simon was anxious. They had been out all night fishing and had caught nothing. Fishing for him and his brothers was not a relaxing diversion. It was the source of their economic stability, how they earned a living, made their house payments, and fed their families. To labor all night and catch nothing was at least a short-term financial stressor. There is always an element of fear in the gut for those of us on the highwire of self-employment with no safety net below.

At the urging of Jesus, they have put out their nets again. This time, their nets are so filled with fish that they begin breaking, and the boats begin sinking. Their catch of fish is a bonanza. It wipes out any short-term financial fear. But now, Simon's shame kicks in. He is afraid again, this time for a different reason.

"Depart from me, for I am a sinful man, O Lord."

There comes a point in our recovery process where we begin to make this transition from one fear to another. At first, our fear is not knowing how to live with the unbearable circumstances in our lives. Our anxiety level is through the roof. Our energy level is low. We worry that we won't be able to muster the strength to continue to function, work our jobs, maintain our households, and sustain marriages or other family relationships.

I remember waking in the morning when it took every ounce of will just to get out of bed. I felt like there was an elephant in the room, and I was being told I had to eat it. I was afraid I would totally break down and be unable to financially support myself and my family.

With God's help, I began to recover, and a different fear emerged: "What am I capable of doing? What is God going to ask me to do?"

I had carefully hidden the fact that I had been suicidal and all the factors that had led to that thinking pattern. The failed marriage, the estrangement from my children, the homelessness, the rejection from my parents, the financial ruin, the loss of friends.

I eventually realized that Jesus was saying to me what he had also said to Simon. While Simon's life disqualified him from admission to the Hall of Perfection, it immediately qualified him to become a perfect fisher of imperfect men and women. People need to hear the good news of God's love from the mouths of imperfect persons who are like them.

When I put my suicidal history into God's hands, it became clear that I needed to begin talking honestly about it. I started referring to myself as a "Second Day" person, someone who had survived the night of suicidal thinking. Some people were shocked. Some family members were embarrassed and ashamed of me. Most friends avoided the subject.

Suddenly, people with lived experience of suicide began sharing their stories with me—hundreds of them. People would come up to me at a break and whisper in my ear, "I, too, am a Second Day person." One person collapsed in my arms. Mothers and fathers shared photos of lost sons or daughters. People who were struggling with suicide at that very point in their lives opened up to ask for support. God has made me a fisher of the suicidally desperate.

Like Simon, I have been disqualified from the Hall of Perfection, and you may have been as well. Also, like Simon, it may frighten you to put yourself into God's hands to discover what God wants to do with your life. What will happen if God "gets a hold of you"?

Ironically, Simon's first reaction was to run from what he needed most: a powerful love that accepted him just as he was and a purpose worthy of his precious life. It may be ours as well.

Something to think about:

What is holding you back from your relationship with God? How can you relate to Simon and how he may have felt those first moments with Jesus? How do you think this would change your perspective? More qualified?

Prayer

Lord Jesus, I have lived with a belly full of fear for what seems like a lifetime. I have been afraid of the pain of living, the uncertainty of dying, and the possibility I might fall into the abyss of a total breakdown. But as I recover, I wonder what might happen if I allow you to truly take hold of my life. Help me to trust that you have qualified me for a life that touches others, not with a message of the survival of the spiritually fittest, but with the assurance that imperfect people like me can, indeed, find a life worth living. Amen.

DAY FORTY-TWO

For we do not want you to be unaware, brothers, of the affliction we experienced in Asia. For we were so utterly burdened beyond our strength that we despaired of life itself. Indeed, we felt that we had received the sentence of death. But that was to make us rely not on ourselves but on God who raises the dead.

-- 2 Cor. 1:8-9

Today's reading turns our attention away from shame as a factor in our suicidal thinking, to extreme stress. It is usually the case that we will need to address several factors in our recovery process, and extreme stress is likely one of them.

Paul describes a situation in which he and his colleagues were "utterly burdened" beyond their strength. This is simply another way of describing the unbearable circumstance that often turns our thinking to death. In this case, Paul thought it might be a sentence of death imposed upon them. For those of us who are prone to suicide, the sentence of death is one we impose upon ourselves. In either case, the stressor we are dealing with leaves us feeling utterly burdened beyond our strength.

Paul makes it clear that he needs the Corinthians to understand the severity of his experience: "We do not want you to be unaware...of the affliction we experienced in Asia." When we are going through an experience that is so unbearable that we begin to consider suicide, we need others to understand how utterly burdensome it really is. When folks, usually out of good motive, minimize the issue that is crushing us or try to convince us that things are not as bad as we perceive, it tends to isolate us in the experience. Alternatively, we conclude that there must be something seriously wrong with us for making a mountain out of a molehill.

"We don't want you to be unaware..." Paul needed people to understand his experience.

When I was in the depths of my despair, one of my best friends listened to me describe the ways the legal system was putting me into an intolerable, irrational bind.

"I am trapped," I told her. "I feel like killing myself is the only way out."

Her response was quick and compact. "Then leave the country," she said. "Better to leave the country and stay alive than stay here and die."

I will always love her for that response. The seriousness of her solution matched the extremity of my despair. While my attorney kept saying "These things always work out," my friend was saying, "I am aware of how serious this is for you. Let's do whatever it takes to keep you alive. You matter."

Part of our long-term recovery will require the cultivation of a community of persons who will take seriously our stressors, especially when they approach a point where we are so "utterly burdened beyond our strength that we despair of life itself."

Of course, Paul is describing an experience in the past. He survived. The Greek construction he uses in his verbs is not directly translatable into English. It is the aorist tense, which is used to indicate a singular action at a point in time. An expanded translation might be: "For an *instant,* we were so utterly burdened beyond our strength that, *at that moment*, we despaired of life itself. *Then, the despair passed. It was over.*"

Stressors come and go. On the scale of an entire life, they are the proverbial blip on a radar screen. As another Second Day person once said to me, "I've had to learn to say to myself, 'I've had a bad day, but that doesn't mean I have to have a bad life.'"

To recover from suicidal thinking, we must join Paul and millions of others in learning to rely "not on ourselves but on God..." There is a necessary gap between our strength and the unbearable situations that place us "beyond our strength." That gap is the gap of trust. We do not have to have all the answers, all the strength, all the willpower. If we learn to release ourselves to God in that gap of trust, the unbearable becomes bearable, and a life worth living comes within reach.

Something to think about:

What are the stresses you have in your life that may be taking your attention off God? How does self-care play a part in this deeper conversation of rejuvenating your soul and life?

Prayer

God of my days, I live in a pattern of feeling utterly burdened and overwhelmed by unbearable situations, which leads me to desperate thoughts. I realize that when I try to carry the full weight of what is beyond my strength, these thoughts only darken. With your help, I choose to rely on you in my gap of trust. As I choose to trust you for that which is beyond me, I feel my anxiety easing, my mind calming, my body relaxing. Amen.

DAY FORTY-THREE

You prepare a table before me in the presence of my enemies;

-- Ps. 23:5

The words "enemy," "foe," and "adversary" are used a total of 1,450 times in the Bible. Taken together, they occur more often than "love" (1,118 times) and much more often than "peace" (812 verses), "friend" (650 verses), or "joy" (590 verses). The word "enemy" or its equivalent is used in 138 verses of the New Testament as well.

The funeral proclamation that "he didn't have an enemy in the world" is seen as testimony to the highest Christian character. Having enemies is seen as a failure. By this definition, Jesus was the ultimate failure, having made enemies in both the political and religious spheres, and among people in every social stratum, all antagonized to the degree that they wanted to kill him.

Today, we tend to think of enemies as military adversaries. In the Bible, enemies fall into several other categories:

a. Persons with long memories who perceive that they have been wronged and have a need for revenge or punishment. Retribution can be exercised actively, through physical means, or passively, by withholding.

b. Persons with conflicting needs that cannot be resolved by other means and only have power left as a solution. Power solutions involve "winning" by physically or verbally attacking someone or seeking to have them fired, dislocated, discredited, or arrested.

c. Persons who seek to distract you from your purpose by criticism, mocking, or withholding essential psychological or material support.

d. Persons with unprovoked, deep-seated motivations to do physical, emotional, or relational harm.

Living with enemies is extremely stressful. While we may not have thought of it in these terms, a significant amount of the stress we deal with may come from persons from one of the categories above. This can be a major problem for those of us recovering from suicidal thinking.

Divorce in the United States is generally an adversarial process, a significant source of stress, and a risk factor for suicide. The risk seems to fall more heavily on divorced men. Divorced men kill themselves at 5 to 10 times the rate of divorced women.

Getting arrested pits an individual against all the legal, investigatory, and forensic resources of the state. Once arrested, it is in the political interests of the district attorney to see that you are found guilty, even if you are innocent. Those awaiting trial are six times more likely to die by suicide than people imprisoned after being sentenced.

There are enemies in the workplace as well. Thirty percent of adult Americans have been bullied at work. Workplace bullying doubles the risk of suicidal thinking.

While we can always take action to make peace with our enemies or avoid them where possible, we must often find ways to live with them without allowing our self-destructive thinking to be triggered.

The 23rd Psalm offers a helpful image. Imagine everyone from the past or present who exhibits the qualities of being your enemy. In your mind, line them up in front of you. Now, also in your mind, imagine a table three feet from that line between them and you. It is filled with food, a Thanksgiving feast...just for you. Sit down. Enjoy it.

In our recovery process, we must allow God to nourish us in the presence of those who wish us harm. This means not allowing ourselves to get distracted from the tasks of self-care: exercise, good nutrition, social relationships, spiritual practices, recreation, etc.

Anytime you feel overwhelmed by whatever forces are aligned against you, bring this image to mind.

And repeat to yourself, "God is preparing a table before me in the presence of my enemies."

Something to think about:

What other verses or sayings help you through stressful times? If self-destructive thoughts and behavior are initiated, what are some simple things you can do to de-escalate the situation?

Prayer

Righteous God, give me the grace to find peace where possible, to make amends, to seek forgiveness, to stay in relationship. But, in those situations where others still seek my harm, protect me from the self-degradation and self-abandonment that threatens to seep into my soul. I commit myself to resist the distractions around me, to sit at the table you have prepared, and to nourish my physical, emotional, and spiritual life. I sit, I feast, I rise, I love, I rejoice. Amen.

DAY FORTY-FOUR

Then Saul said to his armor-bear-
er, "Draw your sword, and thrust me
through with it, lest these uncircumcised
come and thrust me through, and mistreat
me." But his armor-bearer would not, for
he feared greatly. Therefore, Saul took his
own sword and fell upon it. And when his
armor-bearer saw that Saul was dead, he
also fell upon his sword and died with him.

-- 1 Sam. 31:4-5

In contrast to modern times, when leaders send young men and women off to fight wars, the leaders in ancient times fought alongside them. They bore all the risks of combat, being wounded, captured, or killed by an enemy, but also the risk in today's text as well: suicide.

For those of us seeking to recover from suicidal thinking, we must hit this issue head-on. There are certain vocations that place us at higher suicide risk. Having served in the military is one of them. Military suicide rates are four times higher than deaths that occur during military operations. You are much more likely to kill yourself than be killed by an enemy.

When we reflect on the life situation for Saul, we can observe two factors contributing to his death: (a) the stress of his situation--combat, and (b) having the means to take his life readily available—a sword. While that was roughly 3,000 years ago, those same two factors make some vocations riskier than others today.

People who work in stressful vocations with low wages, job insecurity, or injury risk have the highest suicide risk. This includes areas such as construction, mining, the arts, farming, fishing, sports, transportation, and material moving.

Close behind are those, like Saul, whose work gives them easy access to lethal means. That includes those who have access to medications, like physicians, nurses, dentists, and veterinarians, but also those who carry firearms, like police officers, guards, and others in protective services.

How might all this figure into our recovery?

First, it may be helpful to recognize that the risks posed by our vocation are not a degradation of who we are. If Saul had been in any other line of work, it is likely that his story would not have ended this way.

Second, knowing that we are in or have been in a vocation with a higher suicide risk can help us take steps to protect ourselves. It will be even more important for us to practice self-care, good nutrition, regular exercise, social connections, spiritual practices, etc. Using this devotional on a daily basis might be one component of your self-care and self-protection.

Third, during recovery, finding ways to put as much distance between yourself and the lethal means that are a part of your job is critical. I grew up in a hunting family. There were several shot-guns that hung on a gun rack in my parents' home. At my lowest point, I asked my brother to remove those. Suicide would require that I purchase a gun and that additional step is what bought me time to reconsider and ultimately may have saved my life. Given our profession, we can't totally remove those means from our lives, but we can take steps to create extra, life-saving steps that will delay our using them.

Finally, it is important to remember that suicidal behavior is contagious. "And when his armor-bearer saw that Saul was dead, he also fell upon his sword and died with him." Contrary to our fears, talking about suicide doesn't make it more likely. However, acting on our suicidal thinking puts everyone around us at higher risk: our families, friends, work associates...everyone.

We can't always eliminate the stress from our lives, including our jobs. But we can set our intention to allow that stress to bring us back to God, to prayer, to surrender to God's will, and to fellowship with God's people wherever we find them.

Something to think about:

Safety planning is essential to keeping yourself safe. Are there things you need to be thinking about removing or having someone else remove if suicidal thoughts start to come back or occur? Why would this be important for a certain time period?

Prayer

Eternal God, we thank you that all who have died by their own hand are now held in your more loving, protective hands. Grant that Saul, his armor-bearer, and others in stressful job situations might not have died in vain. May we learn important lessons from them and take steps to protect our lives so that our mission on the earth might not be cut short by distortions of mind or heart. Help us to choose life, not only for ourselves, but so that those we care about might find in us a model of courage, resilience, and love. Amen.

DAY FORTY-FIVE

When Jesus saw him lying there and knew that he had already been there a long time, he said to him, "Do you want to be healed?"

-- John 5:6

When we first begin any recovery process, our choices may be limited. The very first step of AA is "We admit we were powerless over alcohol." The same could be said for anything that has taken deep root in our minds and hearts. This is the reason we engage in a recovery process in the first place. If we could do it on our own, we already would have.

In today's reading, Jesus encounters a lame man in need of healing. The text makes an observation that is not made in any other of the healing stories, "Jesus knew he had already been there a long time..." This triggers a question in Jesus's mind. "Do you want to be healed?"

This may sound like a cruel "blame the victim" question. But when we are in a recovery process, and some aspect of our inner life isn't changing after a long time, we need to get honest with ourselves. Do we want to be healed?

One of the effects of any kind of debilitating condition is that it gives us a handy excuse for avoiding our responsibility to discover and fulfill our larger purpose in the world. As we continue telling ourselves the same story over and over again, we become victims of our own thinking.

This is a particular temptation for those of us recovering from suicidal thinking. An alcoholic may start drinking as a social habit that slowly escalates out of control. The same could be said for any other addiction, eating, gambling, shopping, etc. But those of us who are recovering from suicidal thinking are almost always dealing with some unbearable circumstance that has triggered it. It makes for a sad story. It is easy to keep telling that sad story in a way that circles round and round that difficult circumstance.

It is easier to adopt a learned helplessness than it is to begin taking responsibility for our responses to life. If we take responsibility, we may have to let go of some things we desperately want to cling to, the unfairness of life, our envy of others, or a degree of self-pity. Alternatively, we may be holding out for someone else to change before we will decide to change ourselves.

Jesus didn't ask the man to heal himself. He asked him about his *intention*. Jesus doesn't ask us to heal ourselves of suicidal thinking. He asks us if we want to be healed of it. As we take sincere steps in God's direction, we gradually find it loosening its power over our lives.

Like the lame man, we may be surprised to find ourselves walking in health.

Something to think about:

Is Jesus calling us to be healed? What are ways you become a victim of your own stories? How do hopelessness, self-pity, and envy play a part in how God wants to be a part of your life?

Prayer

God of all truth, please search my heart today for anything that might be blocking my intention to be healed. Show me what unfairness, what fear of responsibility, what envy of another, what waiting for another to change is keeping me lame. I give you permission to remove these defects from my life. By your grace, I recommit myself to my recovery, and I set my intention: I want to be healed. Amen.

"The things you take for granted, someone else is praying for." – Anonymous

DAY FORTY-SIX

Now when he heard that John had been arrested, he withdrew into Galilee.

-- Matt. 4:12

The apostles returned to Jesus and told him all that they had done and taught. And he said to them, "Come away by yourselves to a desolate place and rest a while." For many were coming and going, and they had no leisure even to eat. And they went away in the boat to a desolate place by themselves.

--Mark 6:30-32

We are sometimes given the impression that the entire thrust of Jesus's life was sacrificing himself in the service of others. This perception leads us to judge any act of self-care, particularly for ourselves, as selfish.

Today's readings challenge that assumption. They focus on two events related to John the Baptist, who was not only Jesus's supporter but also his cousin.

First was the news that John had been arrested. Herod had imprisoned John in his fortress palace, Machaerus, which was located about thirty miles southeast of Jerusalem. In response, Jesus withdraws to Galilee, about 40 miles *north* of Jerusalem. It is not difficult to imagine why. Jesus is trying to protect himself from being arrested as well. While some might judge him for running away from trouble, his ministry hangs in the balance. This act of self-care is essential not only to him but to those he is called to serve.

Sometimes, we are hesitant to make a change in a situation that is contributing to our suicidal thinking because that act of self-care might be judged as selfish. However, if we allow ourselves to have "the mind of Christ," it may be revealed that protecting ourselves is not selfish; it may be a way of preserving our ability to serve others in the long run.

In Jesus's actions, we see a clear distinction between selfishness and self-care. Being selfish is the desire to take away from others and not give back. Self-care is all about replenishing your own resources without depleting someone else's.

The second event, even more tragic, was Herod's execution of John. When his disciples return from their ministries with their reports, including news of this horrific event, Jesus withdraws again: "Come away by yourselves to a desolate place and rest a while."

However, this second withdrawal is not due to an external threat like Herod. Jesus is concerned about the internal depletion they are experiencing in trying to care for so many other people "who were coming and going, and they had no leisure even to eat." It is an act of self-care, not only for himself but for his disciples as well.

Self-care is the practice of taking an active role in protecting one's own well-being and happiness, in particular during periods of stress. It can include any number of things including physical rest, exercise, recreation, meeting with friends, getting outside, journaling, or getting a massage. We each need to develop an individualized self-care plan that fits our situation.

Self-care is essential to our recovery process. Receiving word that his cousin had been brutally murdered was undoubtedly a traumatic shock to Jesus. We do not know what additional temptations befell him as a result, but for those of us in recovery, any traumatic shock can temporarily set us back. We may begin thinking in ways that we thought we had conquered long ago.

When that happens, it is important for us to be gentle with ourselves. Go back to readings in this devotional that have been particularly helpful and read them again. Recommit yourself to your recovery process.

And engage in self-care.

Something to think about:

There are times when we need to disengage from the world to relieve stress. When do you find yourself needing to step away so God can help in the healing process? Where do you find this place of healing? Are there others who can help?

Prayer

Lord Jesus, thank you for setting the pattern for dealing with threats to my well-being, both external and internal. Give me wisdom to discern the difference between selfishness and self-care and to make the changes in my life that are necessary to my physical, emotional, and spiritual health. When traumatic news comes my way, help me to be gentle with myself, to take steps to heal, and to recommit myself to you in my recovery process. Amen.

DAY FORTY-SEVEN

Blessed are those who are persecuted for righteousness' sake, for theirs is the kingdom of heaven. Blessed are you when others revile you and persecute you and utter all kinds of evil against you falsely on my account. Rejoice and be glad, for your reward is great in heaven, for so they persecuted the prophets who were before you.

-- Matt. 5:10-12

Indeed, the hour is coming when whoever kills you will think he is offering service to God.

-- John 16:2

"If I asked you what anxiety feels like in your body, you could probably tell me instantly. But we forget that joy has a feeling too."

-- Ingrid Fetell Lee

On March 11, 2004, a coordinated series of bombs exploded in four commuter trains in Madrid. The explosions killed 191 people, wounded 1800 others, and set in motion a full-scale international investigation. On the basis of a latent fingerprint lifted from a bag containing detonating devices, the U.S. Federal Bureau of Investigation (FBI) positively identified Brandon Mayfield, an American from the state of Oregon.

Subsequent to 9–11, Mayfield had been on an FBI watch list, and the latent fingerprint lifted off the bag confirmed their suspicions. Brandon Mayfield was arrested. During his incarceration, he was kept in the jail's mental ward, where he was concerned for his own safety. He became even more concerned as other inmates recognized him on the evening news. He was handcuffed, forced to wear leg irons, and routinely strip-searched.

But Mayfield was completely innocent. A few weeks later, the real bomber was discovered to be an Algerian national. Because the FBI *expected* Mayfield to be guilty, they found evidence *confirming* he was guilty.

It is called "confirmation bias." Confirmation bias is the tendency of individuals to favor information that confirms their beliefs or ideas and discount that which does not.

Jesus is describing the experience of a group of individuals who are victims of confirmation bias. Once people believe you are inferior, defective, or dangerous — Brandon Mayfield was a Muslim — they will see everything you do and everything you are through that lens. They will find "reasons to revile you and persecute you and utter all kinds of evil against you falsely," all the while believing that they are doing God a favor.

For those of us recovering from suicidal thinking who are also members of a group seen by society as inferior, defective, or dangerous, the issue must be faced directly. We may be reviled — railed at, taunted, debased. Even when we try to keep to ourselves, we may be persecuted—pursued, harassed, threatened. We may be spoken against as evil--wicked, malicious, lazy.

When we internalize these words either passively (maybe there is something wrong with me) or reactively (the unfairness of my life will defeat me), it hinders our recovery.

Jesus does not give us a quick fix, but he does address our situation in some ways I find helpful.

First, he recognizes the injustice of what is happening to us. We can be reviled, persecuted, and lied about *for righteousness' sake; that is* when we are doing nothing wrong. This doesn't mean we are perfect. It means we have done all we can to be in right relationship with God, with ourselves, and with those who will permit us to be.

Second, Jesus affirms that we are not alone. As a person who himself was reviled, persecuted, and falsely accused, he is our brother. He walks with us. He declares us supremely blessed.

Third, Jesus goes straight to the heart of the matter: our identity. He places us among the most esteemed people of his day, the prophets. Because we are so highly esteemed, Jesus invites us to rejoice, to literally jump for joy.

Jesus does not ask us to enjoy being trashed as people. He asks us in those seasons of oppression to resist the temptation to surrender, and encourages us to reclaim who we are with all the pluck that God gives us.

We each have confirmation biases about ourselves as well. If we believe ourselves to be worthless, we will find evidence confirming it. But if we join Jesus in believing that we are beloved, blessed, companioned, and members of God's Hall of Fame, we will find evidence confirming that.

Something to think about:

What are some ways you can become a part of the larger story of those with lived experience? What does God say about those who *are persecuted and reviled?* Is there a way you can tell your story of lived experience while still remaining safe with yourself?

Prayer

God of grace and truth, I reflect today on those life situations that Jesus describes. I think about those who believe the worst about people like me and easily find evidence that confirms it. Remind me that I am not alone. Remind me that I am in good company. Remind me of who I am. Remind me that there are people of compassion working toward justice on our behalf. Help me not give up on that cause. Give me a heart that believes the best about myself, and others like me, that I might rejoice more and more in the beauty of all that you have made. Amen.

DAY FORTY-EIGHT

*Jesus said to [the Samaritan woman],
"Go, call your husband, and come here."
The woman answered him, "I have no husband." Jesus said to her, "You are right in
saying, 'I have no husband' for you have
had five husbands, and the one you now
have is not your husband. What you have
said is true." Just then his disciples came
back. They marveled that he was talking
with a woman, but no one said, "What do
you seek?" or, "Why are you talking with
her?" So the woman left her water jar and
went away into town and said to the people, "Come, see a man who told me all that
I ever did. Can this be the Christ?" They
went out of the town and were coming to
him.*

-- John 4:16-18, 27-30

In today's reading, it's easy to jump to the conclusion that the woman described there is something

of a moral failure. By her own admission, she is cohabiting with a man she is not married to. The fact that she has been married five times previously suggests some degree of sexual promiscuity.

What she tells Jesus regarding her marital status is technically true, but it is not the whole truth. This suggests a degree of duplicity, probably out of shame. But we already know this about her. The fact that she is coming to the well in the midday heat rather than in the cool of the morning suggests that she wants to avoid the other women who might look down on her.

But there is more to the story than her individual failures. We must also look at the failure of her society to offer justice for women as a whole and this woman in particular.

Women in Jesus's day were considered the property of men, first their fathers, then their husbands. Their identity was bound up in the husband they married and the children they bore. Women were excluded from public religious life and generally not permitted to learn the Torah.

A man who tired of his wife could divorce her for any reason, even poor cooking, with no obligation to financially care for her. A woman, on the other hand, could never divorce her husband. When Jesus said, "You have had five husbands," he was really saying, "Five men have divorced you." Given the dire prospects of a divorced woman in that society, it is no wonder she attached herself to a man to whom she is not married, if for no other reason than pure survival.

While the prospects for women today have vastly improved, they still carry an uneven emotional load in our society, and this burden can impact their recovery from suicidal thinking. Women are three times more likely to attempt suicide than men, and two to three times more likely to have suicidal thoughts than men.

The lasting impact of sexual and physical violence from men is a significant issue. Sexual abuse in childhood is a major factor for future suicidal behavior and can also be a source of PTSD. Survivors of intimate partner violence are twice as likely to attempt suicide multiple times.

Body self-image issues can be caused by pressures to obtain unrealistic physical expectations. Related eating disorders, including anorexia nervosa and bulimia nervosa, also can contribute to suicidal thinking.

For those of us in recovery who are dealing with these issues, there are important spiritual insights in this passage.

First, Jesus is willing to break multiple social norms in order to engage this woman. While we have no indication that she was suicidal, there is every reason to believe that she lived with a degree of desperation. As with other women in the Gospels, Jesus was simply unwilling to allow social conventions to stand in the way of a liberating encounter.

Second, it was clear from her reaction that her experience of Jesus was free of the judgment she likely experienced from other religious men. Most of us would not find it comforting to meet a man who told us *all* we had ever done without feeling a considerable degree of exposure and shame. But there is no indication that Jesus judged her at all, not for her shading of the truth, not for her having had five husbands, not for her living with a man outside of marriage. The burden of shame had been lifted from her shoulders.

Finally, there was the restoration of her self-confidence, her pluck, her zest. The woman who would avoid other women at all costs, even by enduring the hot midday summer sun, is now talking to everyone. And she was apparently quite persuasive: "They went out of the town and were coming to him."

For those of us who are women, these same issues threaten our recovery from suicidal thinking: economic insecurity, childhood sexual abuse, intimate partner assault, poor body image, and the unequal emotional burden we bear in fulfilling multiple roles. We make mistakes in dealing with these issues, and we often bear a crushing amount of shame in spite of the fact that we are doing the best we can.

The same Jesus who went out of his way to encounter this woman goes out of his way to encounter us in the Spirit. Whatever we may have experienced from other men, the man Jesus has come to set us free.

Something to think about:

What depths do you believe Jesus knows you? In what ways do you avoid people? What was meaningful about this story to you?

Prayer

Jesus, thank you for going off the beaten path to meet me today. Please sit with me as I review the insights from today's reading and how the issues in this woman's life have contributed to my own suicidal thinking. As I allow myself to accept that I have done the best that I could with what I had to deal with, roll the burden of shame off my shoulders. Remind me that we all need to be forgiven of something, including the society that has made life difficult for generations of women. Like my Samaritan sister, help me recover my self-confidence, my courage, and my zest for living. Amen.

DAY FORTY-NINE

The scribes and the Pharisees brought a woman who had been caught in adultery, and placing her in the midst they said to him, "Teacher, this woman has been caught in the act of adultery. Now in the Law, Moses commanded us to stone such women. So what do you say?" And as they continued to ask him, he stood up and said to them, "Let him who is without sin among you be the first to throw a stone at her." But when they heard it, they went away one by one, beginning with the older ones, and Jesus was left alone with the woman standing before him. Jesus stood up and said to her, "Woman, where are they? Has no one condemned you?" She said, "No one, Lord." And Jesus said, "Neither do I condemn you; go, and from now on sin no more."

-- John 8:3-11 (excerpts)

The glaring unfairness of life for women in first-century Palestine is immediately obvious in today's reading. It is impossible to catch a woman "in the act of adultery" without catching a man as well. Curiously, it is only the woman who is pulled out of their bed and dragged before Jesus with the intention of stoning her. Where is the man?

Notice that the accusation by these men does not rest on social moralistic prejudice but well and truly on the divine revelation: "Moses," they said, "commanded us to stone such. What do you say about her?" The challenge is terrible.

The literal translation of the Greek would be, "They made her stand before them."

And there she stands. The woman not only represents the unbearable injustice experienced by women down through all the ages right up through today. As Paul Tournier so eloquently describes it, she "symbolizes all the despised people of the world, all those whom we see daily, crushed by judgments that weigh heavily upon them, by a thousand and one arbitrary or unjust prejudices, but also by fair judgments based on the healthiest morality and the most authentic divine law. She symbolizes all psychological, social, and spiritual inferiority. And her accusers symbolize the whole of judging, condemnatory, contemptuous humanity."She also represents all those who find life made unbearable by the injustice and contempt heaped upon them, whose lives hang in the balance with the risk of death, either by their own hand or the blows of others.

And what will Jesus do before this religious mob, with all the evidence and law on their side, intent upon a Palestinian lynching?

Wonder of wonder, at considerable risk to himself, Jesus comes to her defense. To the woman, taken in the act, convicted of sin, dumb with shame under the accusations she cannot refute, Jesus would eventually pronounce with divine authority, the word of forgiveness.

But now, to the woman's accusers, he speaks another word, calculated to awaken their own repressed sense of guilt, "Let him who is without sin among you be the first to throw a stone at her." And one after another, they slunk away. Before Jesus, there were not two opposing human categories, the guilty and the righteous; there were only the guilty.

For those of us who find ourselves pondering suicide, giving up on our own lives, we should take note. Jesus does not. Jesus steps to our side. Jesus upholds our fundamental worth as human beings. Jesus risks his own life and eventually gives his life to save ours.

When we find ourselves tempted to give up on ourselves, may we remember: he never did. He never will.

Something to think about:

How does this story make you feel, and what does it make you think about? The woman and how Jesus takes the focus off of us and on him? What is your takeaway from this passage and your healing journey?

Prayer

Lord Jesus, how I thank you for coming to my side in the face of all that I sometimes find unbearable. Some of what I find unbearable are the injustices of life, some of which have fallen on me. Some of what I find unbearable is shame in my life to which I have no defense against a condemning world. Forgive me for those lapses of thought, where I am tempted to give up on life, to give up on myself. I choose to take heart from today's reading. I open my heart afresh to receive your forgiveness, your love, and your strength. Amen.

DAY FIFTY

Then Sarai dealt harshly with Hagar, and she fled from her. The angel of the LORD found her by a spring of water in the wilderness, the spring on the way to Shur. And he said, "Hagar, servant of Sarai, where have you come from and where are you going?" She said, "I am fleeing from my mistress Sarai." The angel of the LORD said to her, "Return to your mistress and submit to her. I will surely multiply your offspring so that they cannot be numbered for multitude."

So [Hagar] called the name of the LORD who spoke to her, "You are a God of seeing," for she said, "Truly here I have seen him who looks after me." Therefore, the well was called Beer-lahai-roi.

-- Gen. 16:1-14 9 (excerpts)

Hagar is a servant to Sarai and Abram. As an Egyptian, she has few rights. When Sarai cannot become pregnant, she "gives" Hagar to her husband and asks him to have sex with her. But this doesn't satisfy Sarai either. When Hagar becomes pregnant, Sarai is enraged with jealousy.

When she complains to her husband, Abram, he throws Hagar under the bus: he says to Sarai, "Behold, your servant is in your power; do to her as you please." Sarai now begins to abuse Hagar.

Hagar finds the situation intolerable and flees. The word in Hebrew almost suggests an escape from a prison. She is a foreigner with no status, no options, pregnant, and alone in the wilderness. Her situation could hardly have felt more desperate. The only person who has the power to help her is Abram, but to Abram, she is invisible.

For those of us in recovery, the experience of invisibility can be deadly. When a pattern of feeling unheard, unrecognized, or ignored persists over an extended period, it becomes easy to develop the perspective that your own self doesn't matter. This leads to negative emotional spirals, challenging thoughts, and a weakening of our self-worth and self-esteem.

All would seem hopeless for Hagar except for the fact that an angel of the Lord appears to her with the promise that she and her son will survive. (The word "angel" in Hebrew means "messenger.") This spiritual experience is transformative for Hagar. While she feels invisible as a person in her own home, she now realizes that God is concerned about her. God sees her. She possesses spiritual visibility!

Feeling seen is not just about being viewed. The modern tendency to post selfies on social media is no substitute for true relational visibility. No, being seen is more like being touched than it is like being watched. It is the deep experience of feeling understood, esteemed, and cared for. But the spiritual experience of feeling seen is even more powerful. It is *inspiring*. It dumps a fresh load of courage into our souls.

Hagar is so moved by this experience that she gives God a new name, El-Roi, "the God who sees me." And she realizes, "Truly, I have seen him who looks after me." On the strength of this new understanding of God in her life, she is able to return to Abram and Sarai and hold her ground.

It is important for our recovery process to realize that we are seen by God. But this realization may not come to us in our moments of ease. It was only when Hagar was at the most desperate point in her life that she could receive this insight. This will likely be true for us as well. It will usually be at the point of our greatest extremity that we will realize God's adequacy.

There are many ways that the angels (messengers) of God come to us. It may be a friend, a support group, or a therapist. We all need people in our lives with whom we feel visible. They can be angels to us.

But it may come at a time and place we might least expect it, through a dream while sleeping, a thought that hits us in the middle of the day, or an interaction with a total stranger. The place where Hagar received her revelation was named Beer-lahai-roi," which translates to "Would I have looked here for the One Who Sees Me?"

It may come through today's reading.

Something to think about:

Reflect on your life for a moment. Would you have looked here for the one who sees you?

Prayer

One Who Sees Me, in those moments of my life, when I feel watched but not seen, viewed but not recognized, judged but not known, remind me that I am always visible to you. Help me to be alert to the presence of the One Who Sees Me. And in this day, whatever this day has brought me, help me to look for you in this place. Guide me to those angels in disguise, your messengers who do see me, understand, and love me. And make me an angel to others as well. Amen.

DAY FIFTY-ONE

As Jesus passed on from there, he saw a man called Matthew sitting at the tax booth, and he said to him, "Follow me." And he rose and followed him. And as Jesus reclined at table in the house, behold, many tax collectors and sinners came and were reclining with Jesus and his disciples. And when the Pharisees saw this, they said to his disciples, "Why does your teacher eat with tax collectors and sinners?"

-- Matt. 9:9-11

There was an unspoken assumption than ran through the religious communities of Jesus's day, and is true in many communities of our time. When someone disappoints, disagrees with, or distresses others, it is reasonable to expect that they will be shunned or "ghosted."

That expectation is clear in today's reading.

Tax collectors were hated in Israel because they worked for the Roman government and made their money by overcharging and pocketing the rest. We are not told the particular sins that "sinners" were guilty of, but we can assume they were significant, public failures that everyone would be privy to. These often have something to do with sex, the prostitutes, the openly promiscuous, and those caught in affairs. The tax collectors and sinners were representative of the two categories that come to mind when most people think of major public failures: money and sex.

In the minds of the Pharisees, these people needed to be shunned as punishment. This was not simply a personal choice in their minds. If they shunned someone, they expected everyone else to do the same. The punitive power of shunning is only effective if the entire community participates.

Jesus refused to.

Shunning is a form of rejection that gives rise to some of the most painful of human emotions. The same part of the brain that registers the physical pain when you strike your thumb with a hammer also registers the emotional pain of being shunned. While shunning doesn't leave bruises or blackened eyes, the pain is often deeper and lasts longer than a physical injury. One of the potential impacts of shunning is the triggering of suicidal thinking among those of us in recovery.

What makes emotional pain so difficult? Emotional pain is reexperienced by memories in a way that physical pain is not. Physical pain (like exercise) can help distract us from emotional pain but not vice versa. Emotional pain can make physical pain even harder to bear. Physical pain garners more empathy from others than emotional pain. Think of a broken arm in a cast. Finally, emotional pain is triggered by holidays and anniversaries in a way that physical pain is not.

Jesus was a healer. It would have made no sense for him to inflict pain by shunning one day and then go out on a healing mission the next. He risks the sharp criticism of the religious leaders of his day. He refuses to shun people.

Shun is defined as "to persistently avoid, ignore, or reject," but it can take many forms. Deliberately and habitually refusing to make eye contact, acknowledge or greet, take phone calls, respond to text messages, answer emails, invite to social gatherings, these can all be acts of shunning.

For those of us who are recovering from suicidal thinking, it is important to recognize how shunning might be contributing to the unbearable pain we are experiencing. It is no surprise that researchers have observed a high prevalence of PTSD among persons who have been shunned, noting that even being a bystander to shunning can have dire psychological consequences.

Spiritually, it is essential for us to recognize that Jesus never shuns us. "He will never leave you nor forsake you" is the promise that Scripture makes to us. It is important that we take this truth as deeply into our souls as we possibly can by repeating it, memorizing it, writing it, and even singing it.

It is also important for us to work daily on cultivating lasting relationships with others built on the mutual assurance that we will not abandon each other in those inevitable moments of disagreement or disappointment.

God will never abandon us. Let us resolve that we will not abandon God.

Something to think about:

What do you think and feel about Jesus never shunning? How do we mirror Jesus in our community?

Prayer

Healer of my Soul, I thank You for never abandoning me, especially in my moments of failure. When I experience the pain of shunning, help me to bring that pain to you for healing. Give me the grace that I do not return shunning for shunning. Help me, also, not to abandon myself in moments when others abandon me. Above all else, help me stay connected to your great and powerful love, which is my strength. Amen.

DAY FIFTY-TWO

No one sews a piece of unshrunk cloth on an old garment. If he does, the patch tears away from it, the new from the old, and a worse tear is made. And no one puts new wine into old wineskins. If he does, the wine will burst the skins—and the wine is destroyed, and so are the skins. But new wine is for fresh wineskins."

-- Mark 2:21-22

One of the frequent expectations that those of us in recovery experience from others is that we should simply be able to pop suicidal thinking out of our minds as if it were a flash drive plugged into our heads. Or they think of suicidal ideation as a kind of defect that simply needs to be patched while everything else is kept the same. We may even have that expectation of ourselves.

Here is the truth: to stop thinking about suicide, you have to first change the part of you that began thinking about suicide in the first place. That means we must be willing to take a hard look at everything, even if it means reinventing our lives.

Jesus uses two metaphors to illustrate this truth. The first is a patch of new material sewn onto a garment of older material. The patch inevitably shrinks and makes a worse tear than the first one. The second metaphor is of new wine that can all be lost if we try to carry it in an old wineskin.

We can approach our suicidal thinking as a part of our life that simply needs to be patched up. We might gain some relief from medication or other medical treatments. We might find some helpful insights from our reading, from therapy, or from friends we trust. But if we do not change the part of us that began thinking about suicide in the first place, we may find ourselves right back where we started, even more discouraged.

We may have a spiritual awakening of one kind or another, a shot of new wine, using the metaphor of today's reading. But trying to keep everything else the same in our lives can simply create contradictions and conflicts that generate yet another set of unbearable circumstances.

The alternative is to reinvent our lives. What is reinvention? To reinvent yourself is to significantly alter your patterns of living in a way that will expand your zest for living and capacity to contribute to the world. Jesus reinvented himself at the age of 30 and changed the world. Here is what we learn from him.

- Reinvention is often messy and ambiguous. It is sometimes difficult to tell if a person is reinventing his or her life or simply messing it up.

- Reinvention is not for the "most likely to succeed." Reinvention is God's gift for the impossibly messed-up life.

- Reinvention is difficult for many members of a community, including family, to understand and support. Those relationships closest to a person during reinvention are sometimes the most difficult.

- Reinvention does not necessarily make people more holy (Jesus was already holy) or "better" people. By many measures, Jesus was not a better person—they said he drank too much, ate too much, and kept company with prostitutes—but he was a different person with different capacities.

- Reinvention does not necessarily require a religious conversion. Jesus was born and died practicing his Jewish faith. There are many, many persons in faith communities who need to reinvent their lives, across all theological stripes.

- Reinvention is an essential, inescapable process for many persons if they are to decisively deal with their suicidal thinking. It may also be necessary for them to make their full and unique contribution to the world.

Reinvention is not the remedy for everyone in recovery from suicidal thinking. A good therapist or reinvention coach can help with that discernment process.

Nonetheless, here is what we have come to believe. When your life is on the line, everything goes on the table. Changing one's relationships, community, vocation, location, beliefs, values, or spiritual practices isn't easy. Using Jesus's metaphors, it may seem easier and less expensive to simply patch the old garment or use the old wineskin. But you end up losing more in the end.

Through today's reading, God invites us to consider the possibility that escaping the snare of suicidal thinking and finding a life worth living may require some bigger dreaming than we have yet imagined.

You are worth it.

Something to think about:

Reinvention is when something in you needs to die; it is just not you. What things in your life need to die? People, places, and things? Are you ready for reinvention?

Prayer

God, I thank you that my life matters and matters enough to save it from the daily barrage of suicidal thinking. Guide me as I discern how my life needs to change in my recovery process. Spare me from the error of trying to recover on the cheap, to patch what needs to be replaced, to keep pouring my new life into old ways of living that keep leaking it all away. Give me the imagination to dream big enough, but also the wisdom to discern what I must change in my life, and what in my life I must allow to change me. Amen.

"Do not flirt with having a Soul while married to the status quo. The status quo will never divorce you quietly; it will sue you for every penny." -- Fe Anam Avis

DAY FIFTY-THREE

And he took him to Jerusalem and set him on the pinnacle of the temple and said to him, "If you are the Son of God, throw yourself down from here, for it is written, 'He will command his angels concerning you, to guard you,' and 'On their hands they will bear you up, lest you strike your foot against a stone.' And Jesus answered him, "It is said, 'You shall not put the Lord your God to the test.'"

-- Luke 4:9-12

From this distance, it is impossible to plumb the psyche of the human Jesus to ascertain the nature of his self-awareness during the first decades of his life. From all outward appearances he lived a rather ordinary, externally compliant life. There is no evidence of a ministry of any sort, no healing powers, no preaching, no political resistance, and no untoward behaviors with sinful women, town drunkards, or fraudulent businessmen.

But Jesus is about to go through a major reinvention of his life. There will be vocational changes. He will give up his trade and become an itinerate preacher-healer. There will be financial challenges. He will lose his income stream and become dependent upon the generosity of others, including a group of single and married women who follow him around.

Then, there will be lifestyle changes. He will become itinerate. The home that is mentioned at the beginning of his ministry will never be mentioned again, and he will live on the edge of subsistence.

His relationship with his family will be affected. They will come to believe he is mentally ill. His relationship with the people in his hometown will shift as well. They will come to view Jesus as arrogant and self-important in his claim to be special.

His core belief system changes. We don't even need to examine the teachings of Jesus to know this; we only need to look at the reactions of religious leaders to his teaching, which ranged from curiosity to fury.

And his spiritual capacities will change. Jesus will exhibit abilities that were not previously apparent in his life. He will be able to heal people, to obtain information he otherwise should not be able to know, to trigger numinous experiences in the lives of others, and to liberate people who are possessed of destructive spiritual entities.

Pick someone you know well who is otherwise well-balanced and successful by the standards of the world. Imagine that person going through all those changes. Would you not be tempted to say that he or she has totally messed up their life? When real human beings experience this amount of change and find themselves alone, exhausted, and wondering if they have ruined the only sweet life they have, one of their common mental responses is suicidal ideation. Having listened to people in a variety of life circumstances, I can tell you that without exception, people who have precipitated all these crises in their lives share one thing in common: they begin to play out in their minds what it might be like to simply take their own lives.

This is the second temptation directed at Jesus in the transition between these two versions of his life: "If you are the Son of God, throw yourself down from here." It is a kind of test. Attempt suicide. If God cares, you will live. If God does not care, it is not worth living anyway. Jump. This would accomplish the devil's goal for Jesus and for us. It would keep us both from fulfilling our sacred purpose in the world through a premature death.

Jesus's response is clear. He refuses to test God's love. What he needs to do now is remember the words he heard at his baptism: "This is my beloved Son in whom I am well pleased."

Pondering suicide as a way of testing whether we are loved is always a bad idea. I found it helpful in those dark days to actually go to someone I trusted and ask them a direct question: Does it matter to you whether I am alive or dead? Then, I needed to take their answer to heart.

We also need to remind ourselves of the many assurances that God has already given us. This is especially true when we are undergoing the metamorphosis of a reinvented life.

It is here that a journal can be valuable. Spend a few minutes reflecting on all the ways that God has already communicated his love to you. Write them down. Give thanks. Today, we must decide that God does not need to pass another test to prove it.

Something to think about:

Are you ready for reinvention? Who are the people around you to support you through this process? Friend, family, or therapist?

Prayer

God, Rock of my Life, when I am particularly vulnerable because I am going through necessary transitions in my life, help me to stay close to you. Give me the strength to resist putting you and others to the test. Bring to mind all the ways you have communicated your love to me in the past. Above all, may I join Jesus in walking away from this temptation and walking toward my purpose in this world, celebrating once again that the devil has not been able to cut our lives short. Amen.

DAY FIFTY-FOUR

Simon Peter replied, "You are the Christ, the Son of the living God." And Jesus answered him, "Blessed are you, Simon Bar-Jonah! For flesh and blood has not revealed this to you, but my Father who is in heaven..."

-- Matt. 16:16-17

Based upon his newfound belief that Jesus is the Christ, the entire course of Peter's life is about to change. He will see lives transformed, people healed, and a man resurrected from the dead. But he will never go back to the relative ease of simply being a fisherman or hanging out with his brothers, a regular life.

How does a person make such a decision, especially when it will impact their entire lives? What human being would dare suggest such a change? The answer Jesus gives is straightforward: no one except God. No human opinion is sufficient to change a person's entire perspective on their life. "Flesh and blood has not revealed this to you," Jesus said, "but my Father who is in heaven."

Over years of working with people, I have come to realize that there are things only God can say to a person. When those words come from the mouth of a human being, it is almost impossible for them not to sound trite, formulaic, and unfeeling. In those cases, we must be prepared to say nothing.

I am thinking of the child killed in a bus accident; the thirty-year-old hit by a rare, fatal disease; the woman who loses her third child to miscarriage; the head of household on the verge of retirement who hears the news that his or her pension has been revoked; the discovered affair that suddenly ends a twenty-year marriage. In such cases, words wither into dust mere fractions of an inch from the lips that speak them. Or, as Nietzsche put it: "That for which we find words is already dead in our hearts. There is always a kind of contempt in the act of speaking."

And yet, I have witnessed something equally significant. Months, years, often decades later, the loved ones scuttled on the shores of such tragedies sometimes return to the conversation with the startling announcement that the meaning of their suffering has been disclosed! In one form or another, God has revealed beauty to them. Their child, who died at nine years old, had fulfilled her purpose in their lives. It had been necessary, they say, for their son to die by suicide in order to propel them into efforts that would save hundreds of other lives. It was necessary for the retiree to live without a pension to learn how to live simply and open himself to support from others. In each case, they say things to me that I would not begin to say to them. Because the voice speaking has been deep within them, the experience is one of liberation instead of rebuff.

So, it is the unbearable burdens that lead us to consider suicide. I can only bear witness to what I observe. Persons who have passed through the agonizing torment of that experience later discern in it an invitation to some greater depth of meaning or awakened purpose that they would not have known otherwise. This is why a relationship with God is so central to our recovery. Human words can only take us so far.

I have no answers, but I bear witness to this: The great purpose for which God sent you into the world is likely present in the current circumstances in your life. I can't tell you what that is. I must be prepared to say nothing because only God can say what you need to hear next to you.

Something to think about:

When was the last time you heard God's voice? Do you search for the words God has planted deep within each of us? Are you taking the time?

Prayer

God of all seasons, how tempted I feel to see beauty only in what is comfortable, durable, and within my control. And yet there is beauty in every season if I can embrace it as an opportunity to be deepened in my assigned purposes on the earth, to love those placed in my path, to work for a brighter world in dimming days, to learn the lessons of this spiritual classroom, and to immerse myself in the divine experience of this, my human journey. Keep me open to what only you can say to me. Keep me silent when a silent sigh is the greatest form of love. And keep me watchful for the moments when something suddenly becomes beautiful in its time. Amen.

DAY FIFTY-FIVE

Be sober-minded; be watchful. Your adversary the devil prowls around like a roaring lion, seeking someone to devour.

-- 1 Peter 5:8

I define "suicidal sobriety" as the inner freedom from suicidal thinking. I have been suicidally sober for twenty years now. People sometimes ask me, "Are you ever afraid that you will begin thinking of suicide again?"

My answer is always the same: "I will have to be vigilant over my thinking for the rest of my life."

This is probably true for most of us who are recovering from suicidal thinking. There is every reason to believe that we can recover from the tyranny of suicidal thinking over our inner life. But we may never again have the luxury of entertaining just any thought on the assumption that we have total control. Just as an alcoholic must not deceive themselves into thinking they can have just one drink, we must not deceive ourselves into thinking that we can let our thoughts wander anywhere they choose to go.

Our reading today advises us to be sober-minded. This doesn't mean that we will never be anxious, never be confused, never be subject to bouts of self-centeredness. It does mean we will regularly set an intention toward spiritual sobriety, a calm spirit, a clear mind, and a loving heart. When I allow myself to stay in an agitated, confused, self-focused state, I am taking the first step back into suicidal thinking. It is, if you will, my first drink.

We must take an active role in seeking our spiritual sobriety. Passivity is not an option. As our reading says, our adversary the devil prowls around like a roaring lion seeking someone to devour. We must do the daily work outlined in this devotional over the last several weeks, and we will need to do that work for the rest of our lives. But we must not allow ourselves to be overwhelmed by that prospect. We only need to do the work of today, *today*.

A number of years ago, I discovered I had high blood pressure and a risky cholesterol level. My physician recommended that I start an exercise program. I began jogging every day. I have now been exercising every day for fifteen years. It keeps my blood pressure in check and increases my good cholesterol.

I don't love jogging. When I think about having to do it (or something similar) for the rest of my life, I find it overwhelming. But I actually don't have to do it for the rest of my life. I only have to do it *today*. I take it one day at a time.

Finally, our text warns us to be watchful. Think of it as guarding your home, but in this case, the home you are guarding is your inner life. We can easily become so focused on activities and issues in the external world that we stop paying attention to what is happening inside us.

How do we become watchful? By regularly stopping to do a soul-check. What kinds of thoughts have been going through my mind today? What feelings have been most dominant? Am I staying engaged with others in a positive, balanced way? Asking these questions on a regular basis is a bit like daily spiritual hygiene. It is like taking a shower, brushing our teeth, and checking our skin, but focused on the inside.

Having soul friends do this check-in with us can be an important aspect of maintaining our recovery. I find that asking persons I care about the question, "How is your soul?" takes a conversation to a deeper level, which is helpful for staying watchful.

Ask the Holy Spirit to guide you into ways of being sober-minded and watchful that are best for you. I heard a physical trainer give a speech. She said, "People ask me, 'What is the best exercise?' My answer is always the same: 'The one you will do.'"

Something to think about:

What are your best practices for how you keep sober-minded or suicidal sobriety?

Prayer

Protective God, I thank you for bringing me this far in my recovery process. At first, I seemed to have few choices. My inner life was totally dominated by thoughts and feelings over which I had little control. I thank you for the progress I have made, large or small. Help me hold the inner ground that I have taken. Show me specific steps I can take to be sober-minded and watchful. I commit myself to actually do what you show me. Amen.

DAY FIFTY-SIX

He said to him the third time, "Simon, son of John, do you love me?" Peter was grieved because he said to him the third time, "Do you love me?" and he said to him, "Lord, you know everything; you know that I love you." Jesus said to him, "Feed my sheep."

-- John. 21:17

In today's reading, the resurrected Christ appears to Peter. Peter has lost his way. After denying Jesus three times at his trial, he has now turned away from being a fisher of men, and returned to his previous life of being a fisher of fish. The burden of guilt he was feeling, added to the trauma of the trial and crucifixion of Jesus, surely was immense. Perhaps unbearable.

This is the first recorded conversation between Jesus and Peter after the resurrection. It has all the awkwardness of any meeting between two persons where one has betrayed the other in some significant way. How does one even begin such a conversation? How does one get past the feeling that the words "I'm sorry" sound hollow and inadequate?

Interestingly enough, it is Jesus who starts the conversation. He doesn't begin by reciting all the ways that Peter has failed or by unloading his feelings of disappointment. He doesn't want Peter to engage in some painful self-flagellation to prove the genuineness of his remorse. What he wants Peter to do is simply love: "Feed my sheep."

Jesus asks Peter to feed his sheep three times, once for each of his three denials that he even knew Jesus. This settles the matter. Peter is forgiven by Jesus. Peter is reconciled to Jesus. Peter is restored to his position of leadership.

Peter cannot change the past, and neither can we. He will be of no use to the world if his mind continues to focus on his failure. And neither will we. There may be people in our lives who choose not to forgive us. But God always does. For God, the answer to failure is not a crushing load of guilt. It is to move forward with love toward those who need that love.

As people who are recovering from suicidal thinking, we may be in the best position to reach out to others who are suffering in a similar way. Who better understands these unbearable circumstances that drive a person to such desperation? Who knows the road to recovery better than one who has walked it? Who better to serve as a guide to those who are stumbling about, trying to find their way?

There is a saying in our recovering alcoholic family I have come to love: "You cannot keep it unless you give it away." We reach out in love to others, not because we are superior to them, but because we are one with them. By shining a light on their path, we shine a light on ours as well. By sharing hope, we, ourselves, become more hopeful.

Jesus said, "Give, and it will be given to you. Good measure, pressed down, shaken together, running over, will be put into your lap. For with the measure you use, it will be measured back to you." This is the final step of our recovery: to give as much love to others as we can.

I call those who have emerged from this night of suicidal thinking "Second Day" persons. We had the First Day when we never imagined that suicide might become a part of our thinking. We had the Night where those thoughts dominated so much of our lives. Now, we have a second day with fresh opportunities.

There are millions of Second Day people walking around today, most of them holding their experience as a tightly guarded secret. But only when we begin to share that experience will the light of hope begin to dawn on those who are still walking in that darkness.

Let us each resolve to share our story and our hope as an expression of love for them, because we can't keep it unless we give it away.

Something to think about:

What does it mean to love yourself and even those around you? What does it mean when Jesus asks you to "Feed my sheep"?

Prayer

Resurrected Christ, thank you for coming to each of us with your forgiving and restoring love. We hear your call stirring in our hearts to move beyond the past and into a life of love for others. Guide us as we seek to discern the form that love will take in our individual lives. Mix enough courage with that love for us to risk sharing our experience with those who need to hear it. And when we fall, which we surely will, help us to rise again, knowing that you will never let us go. Amen.

APPENDIX A

Where to Turn for Help and Support

Hotlines, Text Lines, and Websites

   Suicide and Crisis Lifeline: 800-273-TALK

   Suicide and Crisis Text Line: 988

   Runaway Hotline - 1-800-RUNAWAY

   Substance Abuse Counseling: 888-997-3921

   Child Abuse: 1.800.4.A.CHILD

   LBGTQ Crisis Hotline: 1-877-360-LGBT

   National Domestic Hotline: 1-800-799-SAFE

   Sexual Trafficking Hotline: 1-888-373-7888

   Sexual Trafficking Text Line: 233733

   Legal Aid:

Local Resources

Psychiatrist _____

Psychologist/therapist _____

Mental health assoc._____

Family physicians _____

Family physician _____

Emergency department_____

Clergy/pastoral counselor_____

Campus services _____

Emergency shelter _____

Domestic violence _____

Alcoholics Anonymous_____

Narcotics Anonymous_____

Al-Anon/Alateen/Nar-Anon _____

Adult Children of Alcoholics_____

Other resource_____

Other resource_____

APPENDIX B

Coping with the Loss of a Pet

Here are a few suggestions to help you cope with the loss of a pet:

Acknowledge your grief, and give yourself permission to express it. Allow yourself to cry. If you live alone, the silence in your home might feel deafening, but acknowledging it will allow you to prepare for the emotions you might feel. Suppressing your feelings of sadness can prolong your grief.

Try not to replay your last moments with your pet. It can be common to ruminate on your pet's final days or moments, especially if they were traumatic. Instead, focus on the life you shared with your pet and some of your favorite memories with them. Remember, your pet's pain has passed. You are the one in pain now, and you must lovingly care for yourself.

Reach out to others who can lend a sympathetic ear. Do a little research online, and you'll find hundreds of resources and support groups that may be helpful to you. Some of these include:

- The Pet Compassion Careline, which provides 24/7 grief support with trained pet grief counselors.

- Laps of Love, which provides grief courses and 50-minute one-on-one support sessions with a grief counselor.

- Everlife Support Groups by state.

- Association for Pet Loss and Bereavement support groups, available at specific times throughout the week.

- If you are part of a congregation, ask if your place of worship offers bereavement support for pet loss.

https://www.humanesociety.org/resources/how-cope-death-your-pet

APPENDIX C

God's Truth about Me

Find a quiet space in each day for the next 15 days. Set a timer for three minutes. On each inhale, take a deep breath, on each exhale, repeat the thought (in bold) for the day.

Day 1. **I am loved, not judged by God.**

"God sent his Son into the world not to judge the world, but to save the world through him." John 3:16-17

Day 2. **I am a child of the light.**

"While you have the light, believe in the light, that you may become children of light." John 12:36

Day 3. **I am blessed, not diminished, at being misunderstood and criticized.**

"Blessed are you when people insult you, persecute you and falsely say all kinds of evil against you because of me. Rejoice and be glad, because great is your reward in heaven." Matt. 5:11

Day 4. **I am exalted by what humbles me.**

"For those who exalt themselves will be humbled, and those who humble themselves will be exalted." Matt. 23:12

Day 5. **I am sent by God to others in need.**

"Peace be with you! As the Father has sent me, I am sending you." John 20:21

Day 6. **I am the light of the world.**

"You are the light of the world." Matt. 5:14

Day 7. **I forgive quickly, and God forgives me quickly.**

"Be merciful, even as your Father is merciful. Judge not, and you will not be judged; condemn not, and you will not be condemned; forgive, and you will be forgiven..." Luke 6:36-37

Day 8. **I have a Divine physician who is healing me.**

"They that are whole need not a physician; but they that are sick. I came not to call the righteous, but sinners to repentance." Luke 5:31

Day 9. **I have a spiritual family of brothers and sisters.**

"For whoever does the will of my Father in heaven is my brother and sister and mother." Matt. 12:50

Day 10. **I have abundant life.**

"The thief cometh not, but for to steal, and to kill, and to destroy: I am come that they might have life, and that they might have it more abundantly." John 10:10

Day 11. **I have an easier life because of God.**

"For my yoke is easy and my burden is light." Matt. 11:30

Day 12. **I have eternal life that no one can take away.**

"And I give unto them eternal life; and they shall never perish, neither shall any man pluck them out of my hand." John 10:27

Day 13. **I have peace in troubling times.**

"I have told you these things, so that in me you may have peace. In this world, you will have trouble. But take heart! I have overcome the world." John 16:33

Day 14. **I have the kingdom of heaven.**

"Fear not, little flock, for it is your Father's good pleasure to give you the kingdom." Luke 12:32

Day 15. **I do the impossible.**

"With man this is impossible, but with God all things are possible." Matt. 19:26

ABOUT THE AUTHOR

Fe Anam Avis created SoulShop™ in 2013 to equip congregations to minister to those impacted by suicidal desperation. He founded PEAK™, a support network for Parents of Estranged Adult Kids, in 2019. He has authored numerous books. He lives with his wife, Shawn, in Hendersonville, North Carolina.

soul🌱shop

Soul Shop is the leading global provider of faith-based suicide prevention training for faith community leaders.

Our mission is to equip faith communities to minister to those impacted by all the faces of suicide, including those who have experienced suicide loss, those worried about a loved one and those who have lived experience of suicidal thinking.

Through preaching, prayer and our outreach infrastructure, faith communities can play a pivotal role in saving lives, particularly in communities where resources are insufficient to meet the need of the people and/or there is distrust of traditional pathways of care.

Through the creation of Soul Safe Communities, churches can be outposts of hope and connection when and where people desperately need them.

Please visit: ***www.soulshopmovement.org*** to learn more about our various programs that include:

- Soul Shop for Leaders
- Soul Shop for Black Churches
- Soul Shop for Youth Workers
- Soul Shop for Campus Ministry
- Soul Shop for Hispanic Churches
- Soul Shop Africa